TEMPLE LEC

THE ORDER OF THE

MAGI

(1892)

Contents: The Religion of the Stars; Governing Forces; Astral Magnetism; Vibrations; The Astral Body; Soul of Man; Infinity; Order of the Magi; What the Magi Teach; Needs of Mankind; A Mysterious Tale; A Mystic Temple; Magical Wonders, plus more!

Olney H. Richmond

ISBN 1-56459-801-2

Kessinger Publishing's Rare Reprints
Thousands of Scarce and Hard-to-Find Books!

- •
- •
- •
- •
- •
- •
- •
- •
- •
- •
- •
- •
- •
- •
- •
- •
- •
- •
- •

We kindly invite you to view our extensive catalog list at:
http://www.kessinger.net

Introduction.

The lectures in this book have been printed together thus, in order to bring the whole into a compact and readable form for general use. Each lecture was delivered separately in the Grand Temple of the Magi before the classes of advancement in the lower degrees. They cover a period of some sixteen months or more and each being complete in itself, no attempt is made to make them consecutive here.

If repetitions of some points are noticed the reader will understand the reason, by the above explanation.

The Temple Lectures are delivered extemporaniously and without notes and make no pretentions to scholarly finish or rhetoric. I ask my readers to criticise and consider the thoughts expressed in them, rather than the style or manner of expression.

It was at first proposed to embody my work on the "Sacred Tarot" and the "Astral Test Book" herein; but I found that it was not possible at present and would make too costly a work, so those subjects are left for a future publication, which will be duly announced in time.

Fraternally yours,

OLNEY H. RICHMOND.

Contents.

PART II.

INTERVIEWS, ARTICLES AND POEMS.

LECTURE I.

Religion of the Stars.

MAN AS A CITIZEN OF THE UNIVERSE.

GRANDEUR OF THE HEAVENS—ON THE THRESHOLD
OF NATURE'S STOREHOUSE — INFINITE MYSTER-
IES — WONDERFUL SCIENCE— GRAND VIBRATORY
FORCES IN PLAY—FAIR LUNA AND HER EFFECT—
THE SUN'S VAST MAGNETIC POWER—TREMENDOUS
CONVULSIONS — IMAGINATION SET AT DEFIANCE—
A MESSAGE FROM THE STARS — THE NEXT GIGAN-
TIC INTELLECTUAL STRIDE — THE GOLDEN PATH
OF LIGHT.

"Behold, I Show you a New Heaven and a New Earth."

THE vast and wonderful strides
made by Science during this
past quarter of a century, has
made possible what would not have
been possible a few years ago, that
is, the re-introduction upon the
planet "Terra," of the old, and yet
ever new, "Religion of the Stars."

The time has arrived when man must realize that he is not simply a citizen of this little

earth, over which the Omnipotant is supposed, by theologians, to exercise constant care, as if it was the only inhabitable world in all the vast universe of space. *

When men first began to observe the kingdom of nature, outside of their immediate surroundings, they very naturally concluded, in their ignorance of the multitude of facts that have since been learned, that the earth was the great all in all, the center of the entire universe; the one inhabited globe, around which all else revolved.

We cannot blame the men of those times for believing that they were the particular objects of the Divine care and that the rest of the heavenly bodies. the sun, the moon and "the stars also," were made for their particular benefit. Nor can we blame them that they, in their ignorance of the facts. should invent or conceive of a system of religion, fitted out with gods. devils. angels and other supernatural personages in accordance therewith. But we are not bound longer by these crude conceptions of early men, therefore we must regard man not alone as a citizen of the world, but rather a citizen of the Solar System, of the Sidereal System, of the vast Universe of suns and worlds that constitute the milky way, yea, of the majestic universe of universes itself, infinite and almighty in duration and extent.

How little can we realize the grand and wonderful facts of astronomical science, without the aid of knowledge. We gaze upward to the sparkling vault of heaven and in its calm and quiet majesty, who could conceive that the shining stars there seen, in the same relative positions, week after week, month after month, year after year, and century after century, were everyone instinct with LIFE and motion.

That those apparently "fixed" orbs are in reality rushing through space, at almost inconceivable velocities; drawing after them and about them their respective families of inhabitable and barren worlds, satelites, comets and meteoric streams of matter, upon great orbits of such length, and requiring such gigantic reaches of eternity to accomplish, that our periods of time sink into absolute insignificance in comparison. But, when all this is learned by the patient investigations of ages upon ages of scientific research, we find that as yet we are but upon the very threshold of Nature's storehouse. We have but pulled one corner of the veil aside, that conceals the infinite mysteries.

Even, when science comes to our aid, with wondrous instruments and discloses to us the motions of these far off bodies and even gives us an insight into their very inmost being, by demonstrating even the chemical constitution of far off suns and systems, we are yet but at the beginning.

For we have yet to learn, that these physical properties are but the shadow, or the cloak, for yet more wonderful vibratory forces and powers, hidden from the view of superficial observation, even as the mind and soul of man is hidden from the scalpel of the most expert and learned anatomical demonstrator.

Who would think, to look upon the calm fair face of our nearest neighbor, Luna, that she, even in her present dead condition, with all her fires and former terrific geological upheavals silenced, yet exerts a tremendous influence upon the earth. Who would suppose from *Apriori* reasoning, that she could not only level down continents inch by inch, by the action of tidal waves; change the very cosmical relations of our globe upon its axis; but in addition thereunto, affect the inmost minds of men, and even have the power to regulate the organic physical characteristics of one of the sexes, to an exact periodicity with her own phazes?

What is the moon's capacity however, compared with that of the giant Sol, who sends his vibrant messages pulsating to us across ninety-two millions of miles of space? Why, my friends, one gigantic upheaval of Solar flame, that sends the white hot billows of burning, glowing hydrogen, oxygen and iron, to more than a hundred and fifty thousand miles above his surface, generates more electricity, more magnetism and more of all co-ordinating vibratory forces that together affect our magnetic and other governing conditions than came from calm Luna in a year. Yet thousands of these tremendous convulsions are going on upon his surface at one and the same time. Amid this "clash of matter" our earth would be but as a drop of water thrown into a roaring furnace, to be dissipated in vapor and gas instantaneously.

When we come to examine more minutely into this apparent chaos of rushing matter, however, we find the chaotic condition is only in appearance, for the spectroscope, combined with our knowledge of chemical laws, reveal to us that each and every process there going on is in perfect rithmic harmony and obeys the exact laws of its existance; Laws that can be expressed in exact mathematical formulæ and correlated into definate proportions with other forces and powers.

Could man, by the utmost stretch of his imagination fifty years ago, have conceived of the stupendous fact that men would, ere the century ended, analyze the chemical formation of flames burning on suns, so far away that the vibrations that bring the message started more than five thousand years ago? But, if he could have done that, by some remarkable Jules Verne power of imagination, could he have foreseen that the message from the stars would be so accurately known and measured that the star's very rapidity of motion and even its direction would be read by the eye of science?

But such is the accomplished fact to-day.

Ah! my dear friends, this is but a begining. One hundred years from now our great grand children will read the pages whereon this lecture is inscribed, with laughing wonder, to think that we, in this XIX century should presume to think that we knew anything scarcely, regarding the universe.

We wonder now, that when Copernicus rediscovered and gave to the world the true theory of the celestial motions, men could not and would not believe him. We wonder now that hundreds and thousands could not comprehend and understand the illustrious discoveries and deductions of the immortal Charles Darwin, as he demonstrated the great truth of evolution. Just so, the generations of the future will wonder that the time ever was when men could not comprehend the great laws of the governing forces, astral magnetism and its co-ordinating mind force.

These things will be well understood then, and new problems will have arisen to perplex the minds of men, and others will stand up before the world I suppose, to be considered as cranks, as a penalty for being ahead of their day and generation.

Physical science is now well advanced. The last two hundred years has put our race in possession of a wonderful store of knowledge regarding the universe of matter. The next gigantic stride must be made in the domain of spirit, of soul, of mind. This knowledge is at present "Occult" or hidden. Hundreds and thousands are striving to brush away the obstructing veil that hides the entrance to the temple of the hidden and Infinite One. Do not laugh at them, or blame them, my mystic friends, as you witness their vain attempts. It is all for a wise purpose, and the time will come after they have knocked at many, many doors, that they will come to the right one, where the weary searches can rest and be comforted.

In the meantime, the occult searchers will go on looking in far off mountains for "Mahatmas" and "Adepts," that exist only

in some one's vivid imagination, and they will
keep on and on, gazing upwards at the starry
heavens with wonder, and they will question
the great unknown and seek to penetrate the
veil of Isis, until the time comes to them, as
it has come to many before them, when they
will leave the valley of Hindostan and penetrate the encircling walls of rock and travel to
the mystic city of the sun, where perchance a
new door may open unto them, giving them a
glimpse of the light beyond the portal.

May that light be a beacon unto their foot-
steps, may it shine upon and illumine their
pathway onward and upward, even as the
clusters of suns congregated along the milky
way that spans our heavens, shine and sparkle
in a golden path of LIGHT.

LECTURE II.

Looking Backward.

A GLANCE INTO THE PAST HISTORY OF THE EARTH.

LOOKING FOR A "BEGINNING" — FORMATION OF EARTH—COOLING BY RADIATION—DEVELOPMENT OF MAN—DAWN OF ASTRAL LIGHT, OR INTELLIGENCE—LONG PERIODS OF TIME—LIFE BEGINS AT NORTH POLE—DESTRUCTION OF A CONTINENT—ATLANTIS AND HER CIVILIZATION—THE FIRST TEMPLE — EGYPTIAN RELIGION — THE MAGI — SECRET SYMBOLISM—KNOWLEDGE LOST TO SCIENCE—COPERNICUS ONLY RE-DISCOVERED WHAT THE MAGI KNEW THOUSANDS OF YEARS BEFORE—SCIENTA MONTANA.

IT is my purpose this evening to take you back to the foundations of knowledge on this earth. Not only back beyond the days of Jesus of Galilee; beyond the age of Moses, the law giver; beyond Confucius, Plato, Noah and Adam; but so much further back that the Pyramids are a thing of yesterday in comparison.

I wish to take you back to the time when the "Light" of knowledge, the Astral Light, first dawned upon the mind of man, and "He became a living soul." We read in Genesis: "God saw the light, that it was good." Can any of my hearers suppose that this is sunlight referred to in the text? Had the Infinite Intelligence just discovered the sun, that had been sending forth its beams for billions and billions of years, as one by one the planets had been thrown off, from Neptune inward to the earth? The only rational conclusion must be, that the light pronounced "good" by the Infinite Mind, was some light that had culminated and arrived at a certain degree of power. Not one, like the sun, that had been slowly shrinking and growing dimmer for ages. But let us go back still further. It is useless to go back, however, for the purpose of finding a "beginning," for there never was a beginning to anything natural. This may seem strange to some, but it can be proven to almost a demonstration, that nothing ever has existed, or ever will exist in the universe, but had something just back of it that was tran:-formed into, or gave rise to it.

So we will begin with the sun when it was an immense fiery globe of white hot gasses, about two hundred and twenty million miles in diameter, greatly flattened by its rapidity of revolution, and was slowly giving birth to a new ring.

This sun of ours has already thrown off other rings of matter which had long since formed by collection and condensation, the planets Neptune, Uranus, Saturn, Jupiter and Mars, not to mention hundreds of smaller planetoids that one ring had formed between Jupiter and Mars.

This new ring about to be ushered into existence contained the elemental matter destined to become an earth and her satellite. The matter composing the sun had, following the universal law of falling bodies, under the action of gravity, condensed beyond the point where the balance was held between the centrifugal and centripetal forces, and thus our earthly ring was left behind. Millions of years rolled into eternity and this ring slowly condensed into a fiery ball from which another ring was left behind under the same action. Thus sweet Luna was born and ran her course as a world, until old age rendered her unfit for habitation.

> " A barren rock is she,
> Fit emblem of death and decay."

Other millions of years passed and the inner globe had become a hot and seething world—our earth. After some fifty millions of years more had passed in explosions, earthquake upheavals and gigantic geological changes of the surface, all the time greatly cooling by radiation, the earth at last became fit for vegetation. Then, in time, animal life appeared, which, by gradual unfolding and evolution, became more and more like the highest type of animal—man. But where on earth was this? All the earth could not have cooled in equal ratio, therefore, some part must have arrived at this life stage before others.

Where was it? I think I can tell.

It must have been that part of the earth that presented the least angle between the plain of the horizon and the great blazing sun of that time. Such a place would naturally radiate heat more rapidly, hence a crust would form and cool in much less time than at points where the giant luminary darted his rays at angles nearer the perpendicular. Two points on the globe fulfill these conditions, namely: the North and South poles.

At which place did life develope?

I might enter into a long argument on the question and quote many scientific authorities and show that the North pole was certainly the one; but the fact is so evident that it does not need argument. Without any question, I believe that the land about the North pole, now covered hundreds of feet deep beneath the polar ice cap, was once the garden of the world, and for long ages continued to be the home of animal life as it slowly evolved upwards towards the highest orders. The length of time this was in the past, can only be estimated by the great geological changes caused by glacialization, which are estimated to show about twenty-eight great geological and astro-

nomical winters of twenty-one thousand years
each—making about 588,000 years.

Sometime during the period mentioned,
man developed from lower types, and began
to move southward, and spread towards the
equator, as the earth cooled. Colder and
colder became the poles and southward retreated vegetable and animal life, leaving in
the rocky beds of the North their fossilized
remains, on their onward march. Thus we
find in latitudes where now is almost perpet-
ual snow, the remains of the elephant, mam-
moth and other beasts; while deep in rocky
strata, we find hundreds of feet of coral formation which could only form in warm seas
during long periods of time.

As man moved southward, there is abundant evidence, that one of the primary streams
of movement was upon a Continent that in
those times extended from Greenland to the
equator, where now the great Atlantic rolls.

Primeval man took with him all the traditions and myths of the past; hence we see how
rich is mythology with legends of the North.
We also notice that the constellations immed-

iately about the North pole, are all named after objects naturally familiar to a wild race occupying the country that they did,—for instance the Great and Lesser Bears; the Dragon, named after the Great Serpent of early periods; Sagitta, the arrow; the Eagle, the Herdsman, etc.

South of the equator we have names of much later origin:—The Cup, the Altar, the Cross, the Crown, the Ship, the Microscope, the Telescope, etc., mixed with names of animals. This has been held by several authors to indicate a North polar origin of the human race. But a more critical examination shows us that even the religions of the earth had their origin among these people. One feature that has prevailed through all religions, of all ages, is the trina, three-fold, triple triad. From the sacred Trident of Poseidon down to the present time the Sacred Trinity, or Sacred Three, has obtained. Says Donnelly: — " The three-pronged Scepter or Trident of Poseidon re-appears constantly in ancient history. We find it in the hands of Hindoo Gods and at the base of all religious beliefs of antiquity. "   (Atlantis, p. 26).

Dr. Arthur Scott speaks also of the universal prevalence of triple emblems, shapes, etc.,
in Yucatan, Mexico, and wherever the object
has reference to divine supremacy.

The Trident is, and always has been, within
historical time, the emblem of the Magi. Its
origin was among the people of the Northern
Hemisphere, and was taken from the position
of the stars composing the Great Bear, popu-
larly known as the Dipper.

This brilliant constellation was then, as
now, the most prominent object in northern
skies. The constellations of the Zodiac were
low in the South and a greater part of the
year invisible; but the mighty Trident of
Neptune was always in sight at night, an object of admiration, veneration and worship.
Thus the origin of the " Sacred Seven " which
originated in the seven stars composing the
Trident.

TWENTY-TWO THOUSAND YEARS AGO,
those stars formed a Trident. The point where
the prongs met and formed a junction was
called Delta. and became the Greek letter of that

name. The star at the junction is yet called
Delta by astronomers, although the motion of
the suns through space, in various directions,
has changed the Trident to the Dipper.

This chart illustrates the changes during
one hundred and eight thousand years, found
from Spectroscopic observations. (Here Mr.
Richmond pointed to a chart and explained
the directions and rate of motion of the seven
stars in Ursa Major).

We here come to the point in human history where the Astral Light was shining in
the souls and minds of men. They had arrived at a point where the heavenly hosts
attracted their attention.

WHERE DO WE NEXT HEAR OF THEM?

9,000 years later nearly, the wise men of
the East established a visible "sign in the
Heavens," that was to be more durable than
monuments of stone or brass.

11,542 years before Christ, the astronomers
of the time had already arrived at such a
degree of learning and intelligence that they
established the beginning of the Zodiacal and
Lunar Cycles.

For a full explanation of the mathematical calculation involved in this retrospect, see " Atlantis," pp. 29 and 30.

Herodotus tells us that he learned from the Egyptians that Hercules was one of the oldest deities, and that he was "produced" 17,000 years before the reign of Amasis.

This and a few other allusions, is all we have handed down to us during all that long nine thousand years. Think of the wars and conquests; the arts and inventions; the slow evolution of man through that long and nearly unknown period.

But let us follow civilization in her onward strides.

About 11,000 years ago, and just previous to the period mentioned above, the first Temple of the Sun, or Magic Temple, was built and dedicated. The Magi had existed as an order long anterior to this time, but had not become sufficiently organized to establish a temple. Mystic time dates from that event in the archives of the Magi. What was the condition of civilization among the people at that time? They were the descendants of that race from

the north who had moved on and on toward
the equator while the continent wasted away
and sank into the ocean behind them. This
gigantic continent had been washed and worn
until its detritus had covered the Atlantic
States of North America with a mass of sand,
gravel, mud, rocks, and other sedimentary deposits to the depth of forty-five thousand feet.
It reached as far south as Missouri, where
this formation thins out to less than three
thousand feet, and is much finer in texture.
(New Amer. Encyc'op., Article, " Coal.")

This shows us where the continent went.
The people, the flora, and the fauna retreated
to that last-resting place, the furthermost
Southern termination of the continent, the
great Kingdom of Atlantis. There the Magi
were born and flourished; there was evolved
the learning and lore of ages to come; there
was planted the garden of Eden, the garden of
Hesperides, the garden of the Gods, where
grew the golden apples of knowledge, that
have always been death to creeds invented to
enslave the masses. There originated the
Wise Men of the East. " Men were as Gods

in those days." Such was their spiritual development that they were as Gods in knowledge and harmony with Nature's laws.

There it was, in this kingdom of Atlantis,
that the four rivers of life divided the kingdom into four quarters, governed by four
kings. There astronomy reached its greatest
development, and the knowledge there formulated was passed over to the Egyptians. There
originated those mystic emblems, painted on
thin sheets of ivory, which have degenerated
in modern times into playing cards.

Yes, those emblems that were held too
sacred to be touched with profane hands, and
were looked upon with awe by priest and ne-
ophyte, were distined to be trampled upon by
coming nations, and become a byword and reproach in high places. Yes; and by the very
peoples that would, with iconoclastic hand,
despoil Egypt's sacred temples, pyramids and
tombs, and use the bodies of her illustrious
dead for fertilizers and fuel for locomotives.

Well might the prophet exclaim, "How
hast thou fallen, oh, Egypt!"

At what time this wondrous land, Atlantis,

sank beneath the waves by some great volcanic, or other catastrophe, we do not know, but it must have been long before the first temple in Egypt. We have the universal testimony of Eastern students that Egypt was old when history began.

Says Donnelly: " In six thousand years the world made no advance on the civilization which it received from Atlantis."

Says Ernest Renan: " Egypt at the beginning appears mature, old, and entirely without mythical and heroic ages as if the country had never known youth. Its civilization has no infancy, and its art no archaic period."

Egypt took her civilization, her religion, and her astronomical knowledge, bodily, from the Atlantians. There in Egypt flourished astronomy. Fostered by her powerful kings, protected and guarded in her sacred temples by the priestly Magi, a religion of Nature, based on Nature's laws, was handed down to other ages. But her secrets were locked with a golden key of mystery, so interwoven with symbols, astronomical signs and motions, that none could read its meaning except the initiated.

This knowledge was guarded so sacredly that it was actually lost to science of the civilized world. Modern astronomers are loth to acknowledge that the Magi knew the true or heliocentric motion of the planets. But let us go back a few years and see what they have to say. Ryan's Astronomy, published in New York in 1831, says on page 235: " The Copernican system, which is now universally adopted by all mathematicians and astronomers, is not only the *true* system, but also the *oldes* system in the world. It was introduced in Greece and Italy about 500 years B. C. by Pythagoras. But from the accounts of his disciples, it is evident that he had received it from more *enlightened nations, who had made g eater advances in the science of astronomy."

Ryan further on says that Pythagoras spent twenty-two years in the East, and " Scrupled not to comply with Eastern customs to obtain access to the arts and sciences of the priests and Magi, to whom almost all the knowledge of science was then confined."—(Page 236.)

THE DARK AGES

then arrived, when every doctrine of science

had to run the gauntlet of the thumb-screw
and the rack.   It was as much as a man's life
was worth to hold to or teach any tenet of
science that did not agree with the various
systems of religion then in vogue.   Under
this harsh treatment the Magi were forced to
transmit their knowledge from mouth to ear,
from frater to frater, under the solemn pledge
given under oath upon their sacred altars.
These altars were ofttimes concealed within
almost inaccessible caves, dedicated as temples.
In time they became even too scattered to
meet in conclave, and for fourteen hundred
years the brotherhood have existed singly in
various countries, such as India, France and
Hindostan.   It was from one of these wandering members that I received the *testa mortis* in
Nashville, Tenn., in 1864.

For several thousand years certain prognostications have been on file, concealed in symbolic language, and thereby recorded in many
books; they have come down to us, setting
forth the time that there would be a great
awakening.   The prophetic time has passed.
Never in modern times has there been such an

awakening of the occult as at present. The whole world, England, Germany, France, America and all the highly civilized countries on the globe, are investigating as never before.

On every side the cry is heard: "Give us facts; give us demonstrations." "We are tired of hearing things that are *said* to have been done in the past; give us something new." To meet this demand various schools of knowledge have developed. We have the Theosophist, Transcendentalist, Faith Cures, Christian Scientists, Magnetic Healers, Transmigrationists. Spiritualists, and many others, coming to the front with numerous converts and oceans of literature. The many novelists have caught the prevailing epidemic, and half of the novels we pick up, deal with some branch of the occult. One hundred years of this investigation will place the world so far ahead of what it now is, that there will be hardly a comparison. Other planets have passed through this stage of development to the higher knowledge, to the enjoyment of the sixth sense. This planet would long since have passed this stage, had not certain changes in our solar system retarded the growth of the astral man.

In this cursory glance at the past, I have necessarily omitted much. I have passed over many interesting events in the history of the Magi. Among these events are the acts of Pharaoh, Moses, Solomon, and many other notable characters, whose histories blend with that of the Mystic Brotherhood. But these subjects must be left for another occasion.

SCIENTIA MONTANA.

Knowledge is like a mountain. Low, degraded men grub in the Valley of Ignorance at its base. Their horizon is limited. They see but little, and think they know about all there is to know. They listen to tales of ignorance of their hypocritical leaders who claim to know of wonders, such as Gods and devils upon the mountain. They receive it all upon trust, by faith. The wise man climbs the mountain to see for himself. As he mounts higher and higher toward the heavens, his horizon broadens and broadens, and one by one the myths and fables believed in by his forefathers in the valley, are exploded.

Broad fields of knowledge and exploration come into his view. On and on, upward and still upward he climbs, over obstacles that nearly discourage him at times. But at last he emerges upon the mountain side into the broad light of the Sun of Science. Darkly below him roll the black clouds of ignorance and scorn. He sees the flashings of lightnings and hears the roll of thunder among the clouds below; but he heeds it not; for far away on the dim horizon he sees more bright and blooming fields of love, harmony and charity. He sees new worlds to conquer; he realizes that, instead of having arrived at a point where he can see all there is to see, and know all there is to know, he has simply climbed to where he finds the field limitless.

My friends, the Mountain of Science has its base amidst the forests and marshes; but its top extends upward among the bright and shining stars in heaven's blue vault, far, far above the clouds, and stretches on and on towards *Infinity*.

LECTURE III.

Governing Forces.

HOW THE PHYSICAL WORLD IS GOVERNED— HOW MEN ARE GOVERNED.

THE UNIVERSAL LAW OF BEING—THERE IS NO CHANCE—THE HUMAN TELEGRAPH SYSTEM—THE GREAT AWAKENING — STARRY-EYED SCIENCE TO THE FRONT — TRUTH GETTING TO BE A FAD — QUOTATIONS FROM MRS. CORA L. V. RICHMOND, PROFESSOR RICHARD A. PROCTOR, AND SIR EDWIN ARNOLD.

SHALL first lay down the proposition that the earth and its inhabitants *are* governed. It seems to me that no sane person can help but admit that such a world, and all that is thereon, could not exist by chance. When one looks about and sees the multitude of wonderful productions of nature, all formed by certain fixed principles, he is struck with the fact that there is a uniform

action at work which causes, in the inorganic
world, crystallization in definite shapes, and
in the organic world, growth in certain definite
forms. Everything from the most minute
crystals of inorganic salts to the highest types
of evoluted beings upon the earth exhibits the
action of the same eternal laws.

A blade of grass or a clover leaf, an oyster or
a clam, a fish or a bird, a horse or a man, alike
show the adaptation of means to ends, the two-
fold division that makes the two sides alike in
form. Why is it that an animal is so made,
that while alike in outward form, as far as being balanced between the right and left, the internal organs are very different. On the outside
a man looks as nearly balanced as a pear or an
apple, while an examination of the internal
parts would indicate that no particular rule
had been observed in the wonderful packing of
the organs. Thus the heart, an important
organ, is placed upon one side internally,
where it does not mar the symmetry of the
body, while the nose, an organ that appears
prominently upon the external man, is placed
in the middle of the face so as to preserve the

symmetry. Think how a human being would look with a nose on one cheek and a mouth over one eye and a chin under his right ear!

While there is infinite diversity in nature, there is also a unity throughout. There is no chance. This can be set down as a fact. We now come to the second question.

HOW ARE WE GOVERNED?

Of course we know the planetary motions conform to the law of gravity; that light, sound, heat, electricity and other forms of vibrating force, conform to certain laws of motion; that the union of atoms under chemical affinity come under the law of chemical attraction and repulsion, etc.; but how came these laws to exist? Why should they exist? Who made them? Do all things come under law likewise? These are pertinent questions.

To the first question the answer is usually given that "God made the laws," but this position is not tenable, for if any being ever made these laws, he must have started at some particular time to make them, consequently there must have been an eternity of time, prior to

the making of the first law, when there was
no law.

Can we for a moment conceive of an Infinite Being existing for endless ages in a universe of chaos, where no law reigned? Certainly not. The idea is preposterous upon
the face of it.

Therefore, we must conclude that. as part
of the universe is governed by law, as we
know, a reasonable conclusion exists that all
is thus governed. We must also believe that
these laws always existed, and were. consequently, never made.

In addition to the material forces in the universe, we find prevading all nature an intellectual force, which, first manifesting itself
in the lowest forms of nature, gradually increases in power and strength until in man
we find its highest expression, in connection
with material forms, upon this earth. Limit
the expression or power of this intelligence,
and you immediately do away with the Deity
of Infinite Intelligence. But can we limit
anything in the universe? I think not. most
or all intelligence.

It seems to me that it is a perfectly rational assumption that higher intelligence exists than that of finite humanity. We cannot admit for a moment that finite intelligence governs matter only as it acts in perfect harmony with Infinite Intelligence or law. You can, for instance, fill a balloon with hydrogen gas, by using your intelligence or knowledge of chemistry. You can then enter the car attached thereunto and ascend above the clouds, apparently overcoming the very laws of gravitation, but, in reality, you have simply used your knowledge to take advantage of the fact that the specific gravity of the gas is less than that of the air, so that the air forces itself under the balloon and raises it upward exactly as water forces itself under a cork or any lighter substance than itself, and lifts it upward.

All laws are universal in nature. Gravity does not act in one place and not in another. Atomic attraction and repulsion can be depended upon always by the chemist. Like molecules always behave the same when under the same conditions. Therefore, it is rational to conclude that if one part of the universe, or even one thing, is governed by fixed laws, all must be.

Thus, we observe that our minds are governed by some action from without. I know very well that it is a favorite delusion, with many that the thoughts that govern their actions come from within, but a careful investigation will show that such is not the case. All our intelligent processes come from some action outside ourselves. Shut a man within a dark dungeon where he cannot hear or see anything, and very soon his mind will give way. Having but little to think upon, his thinking powers will wane, and insanity will soon reduce the person to a beast. Of course there are exceptions, but history shows this to be the rule. In cases where it is otherwise, it is because the prisoner has managed to get some hope, or something for his mind to grasp and act upon.

Therefore, I conclude from all the study and observation I have given to the subject, that our minds are controlled, acted upon, and directed by vibrating forces, from with-

out, and through the action of the brain
under those influences our bodies are mostly
controlled; the only exception being those
voluntary processes that seem to go on regardless of the mind, such, for instance, as
the throbs of the heart.

But we find that even that organ is subject to the mind to some extent, as witness
the increased action when the mind is
subjected to fright or sudden excitement.

It has been known for many years that the
mysterious process by which the molecular
motion of the brain is kept up, and the
results telegraphed along the sensory nerves
of the body, is of an electric and magnetic
nature. Every new discovery but adds to the
weight of the evidence. We might liken
the brain to a central telegraph office, where
the working of the instruments sends out
electric currents along the wires to places far
distant. Suppose the station situated in the
right foot telegraphs to headquarters, " Big
toe in trouble; a hot coal burning the end of
it." Head office telegraphs back: " Pull it
away quickly! " and at the same time tele-

grams are sent to all the intermediate stations
to have the proper muscular motions put in
action to assist the toe in getting away from
the danger. But suppose the wires to the
foot are cut off at any point? Then no tele-
grams can be sent, and the toe might be
nearly consumed without the brain knowing
of the occurrence. In other words, the limb
or foot is paralyzed. We know of no better
term to express the nature of the mysterious
force that acts within us than "animal magnetism," and by that name it has been called
for many years.

On the other hand, it has been known for
many years that the earth was an immense
magnet, 8,000 miles long, instinct with life
and energy, with its magnetic poles positive
and negative. It has also been known to
science for many years that the earth currents
of magnetic force keep time exactly with the
great solar magnetic storms ninety-two millions of miles away. That noted scientist,
Richard A. Proctor, says: "There is a bond
of sympathy between our earth and the sun;
that no disturbance can effect the solar photo-

sphere without affecting our earth to a greater
or less degree. But if our earth, then also
the other planets. Mercury and Venus, so
much nearer the sun than we are, surely respond even more swiftly and more distinctly
to the solar magnetic influences. But beyond our earth and beyond the orbit of Mars,
the magnetic impulses speed with the velocity
of light. The vast globe of Jupiter is thrilled
from pole to pole as the magnetic waves roll in
upon it; then Saturn feels the shock, and
then in the vast distance Uranus and Neptune are swept with the ever-lessening, yet
ever-widening, disturbance wave." ("Other
Worlds than Ours;" page 46.)

It was known to Mesmer and other physi-
cists, a number of years ago, that the human
brain could, and did, respond to the vibrations set up by an ordinary magnet. Since
Mesmer's time other investigators have discovered that sensitives can distinguish the
qualities of even small quantities of various
drugs or chemical bodies on coming into
contact with them.

Ages ago physicians noticed the peculiar

action the moon appeared to exert over the human brain, in all her phases. In one phase, which is only another name for polarity, she was noticed as peculiarly affecting the brains of insane persons, hence the name "lunatic," from "Luna," the moon.

For thousands of years men have kept records of effects upon human actions and events attributed to the different positions of the planets of our solar system, and hundreds of volumes have been written upon the subject, but never, to my knowledge, did any such publications advance the true idea of why and how this mysterious governing force acts, until I published a little work entitled "Elementary Astrology" some fifteen years since. Then, for the first time, was realized the true principal of astral magnetism. I quote from page 14 of that work:

"Each globe becomes a vast magnet, revolving in space, sending forth its magnetic influence to other planets, and not only affecting the magnetism of the inert matter composing those planets, but affecting, likewise, the minds, thoughts and actions of their inhabitants. Each planet gives forth a magnetism peculiar to itself, and, as individuals, when brought into contact with their fellows, receive various magnetic impressions from different persons, so the planets bring their magnetic power to bear on all mankind in all possible combinations."

Thus, I claim the honor of being the first one to bring together all these well-known and correlating facts, uniting them under the general term of "Astral Magnetism," and giving to the mystic force a definite place and mathematical expression.

I have invented nothing new. I have simply arranged certain correlating scientific facts, so that the chain is complete from the cause to the effect. So we need not look off into space to some particular center to find a governing power, or a god to make and unmake laws. Look as we may, we can find no such being, or any place for such a being; but, on the contrary, we find God in all things. Everywhere, in all departments of nature, in every world, in every sun, even in every grain of sand, we find a portion of that great, all-pervading, governing and controlling force.

I set this down as the very last ultimate truth concerning the deific power, the Infinite control. Through all the ages men's conceptions of the Infinite have been changed and set aside by new discoveries. The god idea has been driven on and on from many gods to few, from few to one, but here we venture to drive the last stake, and I defy all the future discoveries, and all the science, and all the knowledge, to set aside or advance one iota beyond the naked truth here set down, that the Infinite Governor of the Universe is a universal, omnipresent force, constantly acting by fixed laws and principles, finding expression through matter of every kind. This principle is intelligent, not blind, as the materialist believes. Every atom of matter in the universe contains its proportion of the force. In fact we may designate the Deity as the "Spirit of Matter," or the "Universal Spirit," with just as much propriety as by any other name.

I quote the following from a discourse delivered by the well-known lecturer, Mrs. Cora L. V. Richmond, in 1889:

Ground Being

" Since the advent of the Copernican system, however, the astronomy of the ancient Egyptians has been revised. Now astronomers are able to trace on the mystical tables or nomes the wonderful truth that science, as far as astronomy is concerned, was known to those ancient people comparatively as well as today." Further on she says: " Even science, in its cold, modern formulæ, is beginning to accept the fact that although the vibrations of light from other planets may require thousands or millions of years to reach your earth; although the intervening space may pulsate but tardily to those vibrations of light, there is a more subtle current of magetism, or a prescience that in some way causes one planet to affect another." (Vol. III, No. 5i.)

Thus the field has been prepared for the great light for many years past by faithful workers in spiritual and philosophical lines, preparing the minds of men to receive the truth, for, strange as it may seem, the facts regarding the universe of matter and its more ethereal portion, its controlling spirit, are so much greater, so much grander, so much more astounding, than any fiction ever conceived by men, that a person must have the mind slowly prepared and developed to a certain degree of advancement before it becomes possible to comprehend it or believe the great truths.

But, thank heaven, the world is being rapidly advanced. Even to-day we find no less than three Chicago dailies devoting column upon column to astronomical science. I tell you, sister and brothers of the light, the " world moves." as witness this in to-day's *Tribune* from the pen of Sir Edwin Arnold, as he gives a graphic description of his visit to that monument of science, Lick Observatory. I can only quote a line here and a line there from his lengthy article:

" Astronomy, I positively, indeed, think, is the chief present hope of humanity, the best teacher of real and practical religion, which will redeem men from the folly of materialism, by showing matter as infinite and as spiritual as spirit itself. ' This is right in line with our teachings and work. Speaking of the church, Sir Edwin says: " Religion had to suppress them (he is speaking of Copernicus and Galileo), or else, as will need to be done, to expand their doctrines and contract their own previous pretensions. At present they have only partially done this. The boldest and truest even have not yet come into step with star-eyed science.

"Christianity itself has not yet sufficiently assimilated Copernican and Darwinian doctrines. When it does it will earnestly thank science for showing how much more glorious it is to be 'least in the kingdom of heaven' than greatest in the petty sub-kingdom of nature which the priest constructed." Later he says: "I repaired to the great cupalo to pass some happy and privileged hours alone with the mighty Lick telescope, and two among the skillful and devoted Magi who manage it, Professors Holden and Campbell."

What a graceful acknowledgement of the services our noble and scientific Order has rendered to the world. Professor Holden, of Ann Arbor, Mich., the same one, if I am not mistaken, was my mathematical teacher many years ago, and I yet have a few lines written by him to my mother, saying: "Olney Rich-

mond stands the highest of any of my schol-
ars in mathematics." He might have added:
" And the lowest in orthography and gram-
mar," but he did not.

But, my friends, think of the tremendous
advance all along the line that has taken place
in ten or fifteen years. When such leading
papers as the Chicago *Tribune* dare come out
with whole pages devoted to science, and
diametrically opposed to the myths of ortho-
doxy. what does it show? Simply this: that
truth is becoming fashionable, a "fad," so to
speak. Newspapers no longer fear a boycott
from the church. No, the churches are like
the late Southern Confederacy —they only
want to be " left alone." They are only too
glad to have science, the "Star-eyed Goddess,"
busy herself in viewing the grandeur of the
heavens, if she will not turn her piercing gaze
towards the dark and gloomy caverns of super-
stition and ignorance. Thank God that we
have lived to see this day, this age of progress.

Brothers and sisters, the Supreme Temple of
Light is ten years nearer to us than I thought
one year ago. It is at our very doors. The

oldest of our members will have a chance to see the glorious consummation. The twelve gates of pearl and the Throne of Grace will be seen by men in the flesh.

"He that hath ears to hear, let him hear what the spirit sayeth unto the churches. The great day is near at hand. Let the nations be gathered, and let the wheat be separated from the chaff, for lo! the day cometh that was foretold by the prophets of old.

LECTURE IV.

Astral Magnetism.

THE OCCULT FORCES IN NATURE.

— ·· —

Force a Concomitant of Nature—Nature's Laws Self-existent and Unmade—Nature's Laws Cannot be Suspended—Nature of the Divine Force—The Infinite Incomparable with the Finite—Light, Electricity and Magnetism—Mathematical Law Demonstrates all Other Natural Laws—Some of the Tenets of the Magi—Manifestations of the Infinite.

— ·· —

HEN in the course of human events it becomes necessary to introduce a new philosophy of matter, or a new revelation to man, it behooves those whose duty it is to inculcate such doctrines, to look well to the superstructure upon which the same rests, in order to be able to present the fact in a regular and graduated order from the foundation upward.

The doctrine of Divine Light in the minds
of men, is as old as the genesis of man himself; but like the science of geology, its history
runs down, down and backward into the dim
and broken strata of the past until lost in ob-
scurity. Perhaps it would be well, however,
to first glance at this Divine Light and define
what it is, as far as we understand it.

THE THEORY OF ASTRAL LIGHT,

or the Divine Light, or as some have named
it, "The Soul in Nature," is, that all things
throughout space are composed of two parts
only, namely, spirit and matter —mind and
matter —substance and shadow — ponderable
and imponderable—or by whatever name
people chose to designate these two states.
Whatever names they may be called their
nature remains the same. Said Pope:

> "The universe is one stupendous whole,
> Whose body nature is, and God the soul."

Each is the counterpart of the other, or
the antipode, but only in the sense that cold is
the antipode of heat, or the positive to the
negative.

At present we call the ethereal part of the

universe " Astral Magnetism," simply for the
want of a better name, and partly because the
force exerted by it seems to partake of the nature of magnetism. and to obey similar laws;
and also because it seems to have its seat or
centre of force in the astral or heavenly bodies,
hence

ASTRAL MAGNETISM

obeys certain laws, and yet is above law, inasmuch as it is law itself.   As the ponderable
part of nature is divided and subdivided into
elements, acids and bases, metals and salts,
solids and gases, and countless combinations
of them, so the other or astral universe is
divided into thousands of grades and parts,
some of which even approach the dividing line
between mind and matter.   One common
manifestation is electricity; another is light.
Neither of these are " things," or matter, any
more than thought.

Let a ray of light concentrated a thousand
fold by a lense, be dashed suddenly upon the
pan of a delicate balance; now, notwithstanding the fact that the ray has come plunging
down from a height of ninety-two millions

Sidhis ?

of miles, with a velocity sufficient to pass seven times around the earth in one second; I say, notwithstanding this enormous force, it falls upon the scales lighter than a feather; yea, lighter than hydrogen gas, or any one of the ponderables in nature, inasmuch as it affects the scales not in the slightest degree. Yet this "thing," which is yet no *thing*, can be twisted with the polariscope, sifted, reflected, deflected, concentrated, and even separated into its components colors by the prism. Then we have but begun on its wonders, for we have its chemical part, its thermal part, and its luminous part; the latter of which we manipulate under the spectroscope, and reveal a world of wonders concerning the motion and physical constitution of far off stars and nebula.

Electricity weighs nothing whatever; it is another imponderable. We speak of "currents," positive and negative, and talk as if it were a stream like water; yet had I time I could prove to you that there is no current in the case of electricity. Nothing passes along the wire except an effect. It has no more ponderability than the thought traversing

your brain. or the affection you feel toward
your loved ones.

MORE WONDERFUL!

and far more subtle and strange in properties
than either light or electricity, is the mysterious force called magnetism. All prevading
and mysterious force! While an opaque body
will stop light, and a glass plate will stop electricity. nothing in nature will or can stop the
magnetic effect. A foot or a mile of glass is
the same as a foot or a mile of air or earth.
Magnetism is, therefore, another of the imponderable forces in nature, that manifests itself through the physical universe. In other
words all such forces are but the manifestation
of the Infinite or astral force through the
realm of matter.

Another law is that the astral obeys and
acts under the same laws that govern its physical counterpart, only subject to certain mod-
ifications caused by its position. Thus we
find that the astral magnetic force acts under
mathematical laws as exact as do the physical
forces. You can measure the magnetic force
of a body as well as you can the gravatic force.

You can calculate the astral effect of the joining together of the magnetic forces of two
bodies as mathematically correct, as you can
calculate the result of uniting an equation of
sulphur to four equations of oxygen and two
hydrogen to form the acid that science says
" has revolutionized the world."

The chemist mixes together a quantity of
chemicals before your eyes. The operation
takes place in the mixing, effervescing compound, look to you like nothing but chance.
It is a mixed up meaningless mass; but, apply
the light of chemical scientific knowledge,
and lo! the mixture becomes a moving, living,
illustration of mathematical law.

Oxygen is here uniting with hydrogen and
nitrogen. Potassium here with other equations of oxygen; then the two compounds
unite; and mind you, not haphazard; no! far
from it, for every particle in the final beautiful crystal produced, is in exact mathematical
proportion. Not a thousandth of a grain too
much or two little. If too much acid was
formed in the process, the potash will not have
it; if too much hydrogen was there, part is

thrown out.   If not enough hydrogen, all the
others are reduced to correspond.

This is the reason why the chemist can prog-
nosticate or foretell what kind of a chemical
compound he will produce under given conditions.   During some ages of the world, mankind, were prone to believe that all, or nearly
all things, happened or came by chance.
They believed that some Being, responsible
to no one, not even to himself, or to any law,
caused events of various kinds to transpire
by mere caprice; no cause producing invari-
able effect.   If the winds thrashed the sails
from a vessel, it indicated that a particular
god having charge of that department was
angry, and he must be placated at once, or
the jib and foresheet would follow the main.

But the astral light still brighter and
brighter shown on the brain of man, and one
by one they found that certain things did
occasionally happen under circumstances
showing the action of Law.   They even
found that lightning, formerly supposed to
be the flashing of God's anger in the sky,
was nothing but electricity.   And then men

had the audacity to measure it and invent
terms such as volts, ohms; and farads to
measure it by. And now we have harnessed
this wonderful power that made our forefathers drop on bended knees in awe. We
make it draw our street cars, run our sewing
machines, and the Empire State asks it to
kill her criminals.

I can even remember the time when it was
common to see a death resolution begin,
" Whereas it has pleased Divine Providence
to remove from our midst, brother John
Smith, etc." Now, some M. D. certifies
that the lamented brother Smith died of
Paresis, and his friends privatly whisper
that he was " too fast," drank too much and
kept too late hours. No one lays it to
Providence. All see that certain effects have
followed certain causes, just as sure as sun-
rise follows sunset.

THERE IS NO CHANCE.

I affirm it and maintain it. As I said before, men have removed one by one thousands
of things once believed to happen by chance.
But they have not carried the process far

enough. Men yet "happen" to be lucky to day and not to-morrow. Men "happen" to hold good cards to-night while to-morrow night they hold all the three and four spots in the deck. Some men "happen" to be always on the wrong side of every deal. Wheat always goes up when they are "short," and down when they are "long' of it. Other men "happen" to always be on the winning side.

When it rains poridge, *their* dish is always right side up. Why is it? Is it chance? or is it the result of law? I say it is *law*, unchangeable and inexorable, that causes these things to transpire. Now mark my prediction: The time will come when men will say: 'Why! would you believe it? the time was once when people did not know that everything happens by law. They actually thought things came by chance."

"What!" says one, " do you claim that things are fixed? Do you believe in fate?" This is a hard question to answer because it involves so much that is hard to explain. It is as hard to comprehend as is eternity, infinity and boundless space. But let us reason on it a little. Every person in this audience, will admit that the battles fought in our last war are all fixed, for all time. All the errors of generals; all the loss of life—the charges and counter-charges, are all fixed exactly as they transpired, and nothing can change them. This being the case, duly admitted, go another step, and I ask: Was it not true, in 1776, that in 1861 this nation would be plunged into a long and bloody war, during which the events would transpire, that did as we know, afterwards come to pass? If you admit this, and I do not see how you can avoid it, you must admit that it is a fact now to-day, that in the year 1896 certain things will come to pass. It is as true now as it will be after the events transpire.

"WHAT IS TO BE, WILL BE."
said the Grecian philosopher two thousand five hundred years ago. "That which is to come will come." tought the Egyptian High Magean 4,000 years ago.

"Verily; I say unto you, these things shall

come to pass," said the Teacher of Nazareth,
1,800 years ago, and it is true to-day, and will
be true when this earth is a cold, dry, airless
and cracked rock, revolving about a dark and
joyless sun, awaiting the fullness of time
when some immense comet, winging its
way out from boundless space shall, unde-
terred by live magnetic repulsion now existing, plunge itself headlong with mighty and
terrible velocity into his dark bosom, thereby
awakening the slumbering hydrogen to new
life, and starting the planet upon another
cycle of birth, culmination and old age.

Everything now existing upon this earth
is the exact result of all the forces, potencies
and environments surrounding the earth and
each part and portion thereof.

Every one of my hearers to-night are just
what they are and are here to-night as the
culminating result of all that has transpired
in their lives, and the lives of others.

Some of these causes may have transpired
a million years ago, a thousand or a hundred
Some of them a few hours ago only, but the
present condition is the net result.

Where will you each be a year from to-night?
Shall I tell you?   You will be exactly where
all the laws and forces acting during the next
twelve months, added to what has gone before,
places you.   Let that place be in the city or
country, Europe or America, on this earth, or
on the evergreen shore, there you will be as
sure as fate.

We will suppose that on a certain day you
intend to start upon a journey to California.
You find from the position and effects of the
planets, at a certain date, that when you are
about at Salt Lake City, you will receive a
telegram recalling you on account of the
severe sickness of a member of your family.

You see plainly a journey; sudden news received; sudden change of plan; sickness of a
female relative, and other indications conform-
ing it!   So you say:

"This being the case, I will not make the
journey at present, I will wait, and save the
time and money."   You do so, and your wife
is taken with a severe case of "La Grippe" at
just the time you would have been at Salt Lake,
had you pursued your original intention.

Now, at first sight, all this looks as if you had succeeded in counteracting the planetary effects and the laws that govern you. But think it over, and you will readily see that you have not set aside one jot or tittle of that law, or those effects. The indications were there, and the effects were there; but under these laws, and acting with them, was, all the time, the fact that you *was* to obtain this knowledge; you *was* to act upon it, and you *was* to escape the returning when part way upon your journey.

In the case I have cited, which is an actual one, happening in the city of Grand Rapids last winter, a closer and more accurate examination of the aspect of the time, revealed the indication of this change of plan through knowledge.

THE LAWS OF NATURE CANNOT BE SET ASIDE.

Not for one moment can man suspend the law of gravity, nor have we any proof that any being in the universe can suspend it. When the first balloon ascended, the ignorant cried out, "The law of gravity is overcome and set aside." But science with her unerring finger

consider?

But what the state of men + woman? Free will?

soon pointed out the fact that the balloon ascended by reason of that very law of gravity. It is so with all of nature's laws.

" But see here," says the theologian, " cannot the one who made these laws set them aside, according to his will?"

No, my friend. In the first place, no one ever made these laws. They are fixed and eternal, as is matter and the spirit or soul that is co-existent and co-eternal therewith. In no one thing can poor, weak finite beings more greatly err than in comparing Infinity with the finite.

Because man makes laws, the ignorant argue that the greater laws of the universe must be made by some great being. My friends, it never took a great being to issue a fiat that twice five should make ten, or that the square of the hypotenuse should be equal to that of the sum of the base and perpendicular of a right angled triangle.

No! nor that hydrogen should unite with oxygen in the formula H_2O, to form water. I firmly believe that ten thousand billion years ago, oxygen and hydrogen had the same prop-

[handwritten margin note: immutable? Law?]

[handwritten margin note: Can Being create new creation with different Laws of Nature?]

erties and laws of combination as at present.
One thing is certain, if they did not have
such properties, they were not those elements.
Everything that ever was in existence, existed
as it did, and when it did, because it had to.

But do not understand me to teach that
human beings cannot act through the will
power; for I do not so teach.   What I do
claim is, that when we so act from knowledge, or will, the *will itself* is dominated and
controlled by the environments of magnetic
forces, called by us Astral Magnetism.

So you see, this governing power acts in
many ways and through many channels.   In
one case, directly on the mind; in another
directly on matter.   In some cases this astral
force acts apparently upon some inner con-
sciousness, unknown to the outer senses. I say
"apparently," because I have never been able
to verify this in my experiments.

But whether this intelligent force that per-
vades matter and space, acts on the inner or
astral man, or not, it acts under direct laws,
which can be and have been verified a hundred
times before many of my hearers.   Under what

Because it
always has
been must it
ever have
to Be ?

law the astral magnetic force acts, with practical experiments, will have to be reserved for another occasion.

It acts everywhere, is co-existing with matter and space, a concomitant and essential of matter? The most wonderful, the grandest and greatest existence, outrivaling all the fanciful *gods* of ancient Greece! The all in all! The great omnipotent, omniscient Governor and Creator of visible things!

Leave our tiny speck of earth. Move outward to the orbit of Neptune, 2,750 millions of miles from our sun. A distance so great that the mind of finite man cannot comprehend it, and yet we have compassed in this journey so small a step outward into boundless space, that we may use this radius of Neptune's orbit as a foot rule to measure the distance to the nearest of our neighbor suns.

But when we have passed on and on, past whirling systems on systems of bright suns moving with a velocity a hundred times that of light, we come at last after many years to the boundry of our universe of suns, our sidereal system.

ARE WE NOW AT THE END OF LAW?

No! For, gazing outward from our frontiers, we behold in all directions systems of suns and worlds, across vast gulfs of space so great—

> That light, in rapid flight
> Of fourteen billion miles per day,
> Starting a million years ago,
> Yet flashes on its weary way.

But have we gazed beyond the ken of astral law? No! For through all the vast and grand realms of matter, whirling in storms and cyclones of suns in yonder mighty space, we still observe the action of the same gravatic, electric, magnetic and other forces constituting the visible manifestation of the Infinite.

LECTURE V.

Vibrations.

LIFE AND MOTION IN NATURE.

THE NATURE OF ASTRAL MAGNETISM — LAWS OF
VIBRATORY FORCE. VIBRATION IN ELECTRICITY,
HEAT, ETC.— NATURE'S LAWS INCLINE TOWARD
SIMPLICITY—CONSERVATION OF ENERGY. CORRE-
LATION OF FORCES. THE BORDER-LAND BE-
TWEEN PHYSICAL AND SPIRITUAL—HARMONY AND
INHARMONY. DISEASE CURED BY CHANGE IN VI-
BRATION— FAITH CURES EXPLAINED--PLANETARY
POWERS. LAWS OF MESMERISM, HYPNOTISM, ETC.
THE MULTIPLE TELEGRAPH -- CO-ORDINATION
OF ANIMAL AND VEGETABLE LIFE. CENTERS OF
VIBRATION. SPACE, INSTINCT WITH LIFE. POWER,
AND INTELLIGENCE.

NE of my previous lectures
treated somewhat of Astral Magnetism, the great and wonderful
manifestation of Divine Power within and through physical nature.
This evening I purpose giving you a
deeper insight into the workings of this force

and endeavor to tell you how it works. The poet hath said:

"Know, then, thyself; presume not God to scan,
The proper study of Mankind is man."

This is all right, and conveys an excellent lesson to those who neglect the physical man while absorbed in the contemplation of the spiritual. But if --

"The Universe is one stupendous whole,
Whose body nature is, and God the soul."

it must perforce follow, that we cannot study the subject of man and his relations with the forces that govern him, without embracing in our studies more or less of the attributes of the Infinite.

WHAT IS THE NATURE OF ASTRAL MAGNETISM?

I can answer that question in few words. It is simply *Vibrations.* This may be surprising to some of you, but to the majority it is a well known fact, doubtless, that all the manifestations of the Divine power as exemplified through physical nature are through vibrations.

I am well aware that the human mind tends toward the romantic and impractical in accounting for these manifestations, and many may feel that this explanation is too commonplace and simple; but I ask you to remember that our knowledge of law and nature's forces tends constantly towards simplicity. I will lay down this law:

"Every atom in the universe is in a state of constant vibration, and each atom communicates this rate of vibration to surrounding atoms."

Then follows the second law: "Every imponderable force in the universe is in a state of vibration, and when such vibration ceases the force comes to an end."

The third law is this: "The vibrating forces change from one to another, upon a change of the rate or direction of the vibrations."

These changes constitute what is called the

CONSERVATION OF ENERGY.

Like every thing else in nature, these imponderable forces can be understood without much effort up to a certain height, beyond which men are prone to deny the properties because they cannot comprehend them; but we must all remember that the Infinite is not bound by man's finite understanding.

EXAMPLES OF VIBRATORY FORCE.

My voice is now causing air vibrations to
convey my words to your ears. The electric
light that enables you to see me, comes from
the vibrations set up in a film of carbon as
frail as a lady's lace handkerchief. The electric pulsations causing this phenomena, are
thrown into the line wires by the magnetic
vibrations of the magnets of the dynamos.

But what moves the dynamos? We are now
back to matter again. The expansive force of
steam moves the machinery and this force is
generated by vibrations set up in the water in
the boilers, which drives each atom of water
farther and farther assunder until a small
amount of water forms a large amount of
steam. This result is attained through the
heat vibrations caused by the unlocking of the
energy stored up in coal. The coal is the result
of vibratory force that was set up in the sap
and fibre of trees millions of years ago. These
vibrations were caused by the heat, light,
chemical and magnetic vibrations thrown
across ninety-two millions of miles of space,
from that stupendous orb that holds our solar

system in hand and guides our little earth and her sister planets, satellites and comets through heir grand enormous orbit, consuming over nineteen million years of time.

The rate of vibration determines the effect.

Thus a certain number of vibrations per second gives us a musical tone in lower C. A multiple of this number gives the tone of high C. These are so accurate that logarithms have been constructed to give exact mathematical expression to the musical scale.

Again, a certain number of millions of vibrations per second causes that lady's dress to appear red; another rate, causes this one to look blue, and so on for all the colors and shades of color known to nature. We find that vibratory force has analogous properties, although so wonderfully diverse in its action.

Thus, take the case of a telephone; here we have an example where the air vibrations cause a metal diaphragm to vibrate, which in turn causes magnetic vibration in a magnet that causes electric vibration in the line wire. At the other end of the line, the entire process is reversed and the message received as sound vibration on the tympanum of the listening ear.

Now, suppose the music of a cornet band is received over the wire. We have the sound vibrations of all the various instruments from the E-flat cornet down to the base drum, faithfully copied and transmitted through all these complicated changes, and so perfect, that you can pick out the particular vibrations of any one instrument from the mass.

As an analogue to this, take light. The pencil of rays comes to us as a whole mass of vibrations, apparently mixed in inextricable confusion; but each set of vibrations are there in perfect harmony, as we can prove by the prism or diffraction grating, either of which will separate the vibrations and assort them so thoroughly that we can tell by spectroscopic observation the very chemical constitution of far off suns, and even measure their rate of motion. This is a triumph of modern applied science so great as to fairly paralyze the understanding. All this is but the A B C of vibratory dynamics however. We must now delve deeper into the occult powers of this mysterious force.

We have now arrived at the border-land between the physical and the spiritual, so to speak. We have arrived at the line where the magnetic vibrations are transformed into thoughts, actions and words.

WHAT IS LOVE AND HATE?

Shall I tell you? Love is harmonic vibrations of the astro-magnetic forces. Hate is inharmonic vibrations. Health is harmony; sickness, inharmony. Restore harmony and you restore health. It matters not by what means the harmonic vibrations are restored, whether by the calming influence of prayer, faith, or Christian Science; the magnetic passes of the vitapathic physician; the bath or pack of the hydropathist; the electric currents of the galvanic or magneto electric batteries; the heroic dose of the allopathic physician; the attenuated high potency of the homœopathist; or the mathematically constructed and therefore potent doses of the astro-magnetic remedies. All of these various schools of practice have their cures recorded. All are at times successful, and, alas! all are at times quite as unsuccessful.

THE REASON WHY.

Because these various processes have been used haphazard, without a philosophical knowledge of how and why they work. The religionist vainly supposes that the Infinite Controller of Universes deigns to put forth a helping hand at his request and prayer for a cure. He feels better, perhaps recovers entirely from a fever, let us say. But what has happened? He has simply, by concentration of his mind, and the calmness of faith, as he lifts his eyes heavenward, caused the vibrations of his vito-magnetic currents to correspond to the magnetic vibrations of Venus instead of Mercury; or, perhaps, of Uranus instead of Saturn. It may be a compound vibration representing both, as the case may be.

The faith cures, mind cures, etc., of the Christian Scientists, Vitapathists, Transcendentalists, and many other schools, too numerous to particularize, all perform their cures by this same power. Does any physician of the old school practice pretend to understand *why* it is that one medicine affects the kidneys, another the liver, another the heart, and so on?

Is there a physician that is satisfied with the administration of the standard remedies? Are they not one and all reaching out constantly after every new thing that is introduced?

My friends, I can answer this, as a chemist and druggist of nearly a quarter of a century practice. I tell you, that the new drugs being constantly introduced and prescribed by our physicians number so many that the druggists can hardly keep track of them. The physician is not to blame for this state of things. He knows far better than those outside the profession do, that medicine is

NOT A SCIENCE YET.

He knows that where he gets the one good effect he strives for, he gets a host of bade ffects following. His experience has taught him that his nervines first " quiet the nerves" and then shatter them. Bromide of potassium quiets the aching, throbbing head firstly, and produces disorganization of the nerves of the stomach that lays the foundation for innumerable future headaches. His purgatives, while affording temporary relief to the overburdened system, produce constipation afterwards. His stimulants are followed by prostration. His quinine and antipyrin, given with great hopes and in heroic doses, to cure *La grippe* last winter, were followed by the total collapse of many physical systems, whereby pneumonia and consumption hastened thousands to the "Summer-land" before their allotted time.

The educated physician knows this to be a fact, so he constantly strives, studies and experiments, in the hope of finding at last *some* remedy that he can rely upon. I am speaking particularly now of honest, conscientious physicians, that really have the good of humanity at heart, and not those who, I am sorry to say, care only to relieve the patient temporarily, for the "money there is in it," regardless of the future sufferings of the patient. I trust there are not many such in the honorable profession,

Now why is this state of things?

I believe it is because every plant that grows, and every mineral salt that is formed by the chemist, has its vibratory power, and is capable of setting up in the human system corresponding vibrations. Administer just enough, and you get the proper vibration to cause harmony; but on the other hand, a large quantity administered sets up too many vibrations, and bad effects, or inharmony follows.

Again, experience shows that the same medicine that cures one, does not cure another: or, as the old saying goes, " What is one man's meat is another man's poison." Besides, the same medicine effects a cure on a certain person at one time, and fails on him at another, when he has the same disease.   Why is this?

It is because of the different planetary effects, and therefore different magnetic vibrations in various persons, and in the same person under differing aspects.

HOW DO WE KNOW THESE THINGS?

1. We know them by recorded observations extending over many years.

2. By knowledge received from a source I am not at present at liberty to divulge.

3. Because we have succeeded in measuring the number of vibrations within a given time, of many of these forces.

Sound, light, electric, magnetic, heat, chemical, and many other vibratory forces have been measured already by the scientist, and we have on record also the number of vibrations per second of the astral magnetism of all the planets and the sun. These measures of vibration, mathematically expressed and co-ordinated with the arithmetical expressions of the polar angles of the earth at all parts of its orbit, for all months, days, and other divisions of time, constitute the astral logarithms used in heliocentric astrology, and the numbers known as the " Powers of the planets."

It is observable that the planets nearest alike in general effects have the nearest rate of vibration. Thus Mercury, with nine hundred and ninety-four thousand three hundred and fifty-six, and Venus with nine hundred and sixty-four thousand two hundred and twenty-four are nearly alike, and yet do not coincide. Mercury gives passion, and Venus platonic love. The two combined give a power of one million nine hundred and fifty-eight thousand five hundred and eighty, which number constitutes the expression of perfect sexual love. But, on the other hand, Mars has a power of five hundred and forty-two thousand three hundred and

seventy-six, and Jupiter of four hundred and
eighty-two thousand one hundred and twelve.
The former representing hate and its co-ordinate
qualities. The latter the love of money and
power.

I will call your attention to the curious fact
that Venus co-ordinates in magnetic vibrations
with Jupiter, being exactly double in number.
This explains the fact that love of money becomes so mixed up with our love affairs that it
is sometimes very difficult to separate them.

The gentle heiress is made to believe that her
suitor loves her with a magnetic force of one
million nine hundred and fifty-eight thousand
five hundred and eighty, when alas! it is but
the combined one million twenty-four thousand
four hundred and eighty-eight of Jupiter and
Mars. Of course you must understand that
these figures are only given for purposes of
comparison and illustration. You must understand that no person could receive the effect at
one time of three planets, to the exclusion
of the effects of all the others. But remember,
that, as in my illustration of the vibrations of
the telephone, as the ear can single out the vi-

brations caused by the bass drum, from the mass of vibrations of sound, so the astral body of a person can single out and respond to certain astro-magnetic vibrations. I might illustrate this by instancing the case of the multiform telegraph. You are all familiar with the astonishing fact that eight separate and distinct messages can be sent pulsating over an electric wire at one time. Why don't these various expressions of intelligent vibratory force get mixed?

What if one message, going to Chicago, says to a broker:

"Buy ten thousand bushels of wheat for my account.—J. SMITH."

At the same instant another passes over the same wire with the message :

"Ten-pound boy, last night. Sarah Jane doing well.—J. Jones."

What is to hinder the mixing up of the baby with the wheat, or Sarah Jane with the broker, or getting them so mixed up that no man could determine whether Smith was the happy father, and Jones wanted to speculate on the Chicago board in "No. 1 Spring," or *vice versa?*

I will tell you. It is all on the account of the same law that I have mentioned. The electrician explains it by the difference in "tentions" and "resistance." But these expressions are only convenient terms for expressing the vibratory force. In case of the telephone it is obvious to all. In the other case, it is more obscure, or "occult," but it is there just the same, and just as truly as before.

ANOTHER GREAT LAW OF NATURE

is that animal and vegetable life are co-ordinated wonderfully in growth, life and decay. As a man absorbs to himself certain effects, and becomes a certain kind of a man under these effects, so a certain plant absorbs to itself certain qualities or certain magnetic effects, and rejects certain others.

For instance, plant deadly nightshade and foxglove in the same soil, and water them with the same water until they mature. The first produces the medicine called Belladonna, which corresponds to Saturn in Pisces, while the second is Digitalis, corresponding to Mercury in Leo.

Plant two boys in Grand Rapids. Feed them on the same food; water them with the same Grand river water, and one may grow up a rich nabob, corresponding to Jupiter in Capricornus; and the other a poor clerk corresponding to Uranus in Libra. The clerk may be the smarter man of the two, but he has got the wrong number of vibrations per second. He is tured to one flat instead of four sharps. He sends the message regarding the boy; the other sends the one regarding the wheat. The former guaged to low tension, the latter to high, consequently they do not get mixed like the babies in Pinafore.

How many times we meet cases where severe illness is cured by a simple change of vibration in the magnetism, caused, perhaps, by the receipt of joyful news, the presence of some loved one, or some other occurrence acting through the mind.

On the other hand, how many cases of illness have resulted from the lowering of the magnetic tone through the receipt of bad news, frights, or other similar occurrences.

In fact, the inner or astral man is *the man*.

and the one who responds to the magnetic
influences surrounding him.   But this inner
man manifests himself through the visible
outer or physical man, just as the Infinite
manifests or becomes visible through the
physical universe.

What can be gained by denying the existence of either one of the parts to this simple
dual nature. I am wholly unable to understand; or of claiming a more complicated
state of existence on the other hand.

The materialist denies the existance of the
astral man in toto. and only believes in the
physical body.   The Christian Scientist ad-
mits the *spiritual* man, but unaccountably
denies the existence of the physical man,
and, in fact, the entire material universe.
But our good friends, the Theosophists, come
forward and outdo the entire lot, including
the orthodox Christian with his three times
one is one arthmetic, by believing in some
six or seven parts to man.

MESMERISM AND VIBRATION.

Do any of my hearers understand why it
is that a mesmerizer when exhibiting his

power will usually try about seven persons before he finds one over whom he has any amount of control?

The vibratory theory explains this also. It is because the operator must find a person whose magnetic vibrations are a multiple of his own, and *fewer in number*. It therefore follows that the higher the operator's magnetic tone, the more subjects he will find among a given number of persons. This is also true of all the co-ordinate branches, such as psychology, vitapathy, hypnotic suggestion and mind cure. Let a magnetic physician undertake to cure a person whose magnetic vibrations are two to his one, or three to his one, and he will fail every time. Let him undertake a case where the patient has four to his five and he will partially succeed only. This is because only one vibration in twenty coincides.

THE RULE IS THIS.

If the number of the patient will not divide evenly into that of the operator, multiply the numbers together.

This rule gives the ratio of success.

But suppose the rate is even—one to one.
We get the formula, "one times one are one."
And they *are* one, in soul and body. In
such a case, if the physician and patient
are of the opposite sex, they will fall dead
in love with each other a dozen times where
a cure will be affected once. The one case
of cure is a nervous state of the system.
which is soothed and quieted by the mere
presence of the loved one.

The vibratory theory explains all the
various potencies and powers in creation.
In fact, I believe it to be the key that unlocks the great secrets of Nature.

It explains the nature of love, hate, friendship, passion, sickness, mediumship, mesmerism, chemical combination, heat, light,
electricity, and in short, everything, when
properly understood.

The subject of Botanical vibratory law
would alone fill a volume. The subject of
Sarcognomy, so ably presented by that vet-
eran scientist, Prof. J. R. Buchanan, together with the facts of vibratory centers, or
centers of vibration, in the cranium and

body, corresponding and responding to the planetary vibrations of like magnitude,would fill another large volume.

I have only touched upon the great truths connected with this subject. I cannot do more in a single lecture. But this intelligent audience will supply the missing links from their own intuitive knowledge of occult things.

As you gaze upward and outward into the vast expanse of heavenly space, and view the millions on millions of suns, speeding upon their pathways around their far off centers of attraction, you will realize that all, all, is instinct with life, motion, vibration and wonderful power. You will think of the glorious and grand fact, that all that vast_ ness of infinitude is filled with vibratory force; exerting its power at all angles and in all directions.

And yet you will realize, that in all, and through all, commingling with every particle of matter and occupying every inch of space, there palpitates and throbs a grander, higher intellectual force that we name, INFINITY!

The Astral Body.

THE INNER LIFE OR THE SOUL OF MAN AN EVOLUTION, LIKE THE PHYSICAL BODY.

THE RESURECTION THEORY—THE RUIN OF EGYPT—
FALLACIOUS THEORIES OF CREATION OF SOULS—
NO "BEGINNINGS" POSSIBLE UNION OF SOUL
FORCES—PRACTICAL ILLUSTRATION WITH CHEMI-
CALS—INTELLIGENCE FOUND EVEN IN THE VEGE-
TABLE KINGDOM—ALL "PROGRESSIVE THINKERS."

NO one question has been considered, in all ages of the world, as of
such vast importance to man as
that of the human soul, its origin,
its destiny, its status in the future,
and everything connected therewith. What can be of greater importance to
man? Admitting that the house we are living

in at present is of great interest to us, and should not be neglected, yet as the time approaches to all of us when we must give up our lease and vacate the premises, we very naturally look more and more forward to our place of future residence.

This feeling, which prevades all classes of men, has been taken advantage of by interested parties in all ages of the world to enslave the masses and subjugate them to self-appointed rulers, leaders, priests and ministers. Elaborate theories regarding the soul have been gotten up and promulgated in so-called " holy books," and preached from hundreds of thousands of pulpits, until the average man can hardly tell what he does or does not believe.

No other question has had so much falsehood propagated concerning it as has this one. None other has had such cranky and wholly untenable and impossible theories advanced, as solemn truth, regarding it.

Probably one of the most unreasonable notions that has ever been held, and one that has done more harm than any other, is one that had its origin away back among the lowest, most ignorant and degraded races of mankind, and has prevailed among various nations even up to this enlightened age, is the belief that the physical body, made wholly of earthly chemical elements, as it is, lives in the great hereafter.

In the latter days of Egypt and her contemporaries, when chemical laws were so little understood, it is not to be wondered at that the raising and rehabiliment of the physical body should be believed in. But now, when chemistry has demonstrated a thousand times over that the flesh and bones of man are resolved and decomposed into their original elements, and enter into new combinations with later vegetable and animal existences, it seems passing strange and unaccountable that any sane person should believe such theories.

This scheme of a future existence was the fall of Egypt, as she gradually spent all her forces in embalming and preserving the bodies of her dead, and the placing of costly ornaments and treasures in her tombs for the future use of the departed.

Our modern churches still recognize this

ancient belief in their creeds, but it is notice-able that they have evoluted to such an extent that, like the doctrine of an endless hell of brimstone and fire, the theory of the saving of the physical body is kept in the background as much as possible.

The second great belief is that of the Mater-ialist, who believes that there is no spirit, soul or astral body, no intelligence or intelligent force outside of the physical, in the universe. This school is the natural result of the reaction against the crude beliefs regarding the soul held by men in past times and even in the present.

As a rule, the Materalist is an honest upright person, and when his reasoning powers show him the absurdity of the doctrines usually taught regarding the soul or spirit and the nature of God he rushes to the opposite ex-treme and discards the whole idea of a future existence, or of an infinite intelligence, and asserts that "death ends all."

"The soul has a beginning when a baby is born." says he, " therefore it must end when the baby dies." This is a good sound, argu-

ment; for who can conceive of a finite begining becoming infinite in duration. The stick
that has one end has another somewhere.

The only fault with this argument is that
its premise is incorrect. It is like the argument of the church. Thus: "Here is a watch;
it must have had a maker. Here is a man; how
came he here? Born of his mother and
father, we admit, but there must have been a
first man, and a first woman; now who made
them? Ha! I've got you there, you don't
know. Well, I don't mind telling you. God
did that. He made Adam out of the dust of
the earth, and his wife out of a rib."

This argument was a settler for ages and
ages, but one day a thinker named Darwin
came along and knocked the whole house of
cards topsy-turvy by showing that there never
was a "first man" on the earth. He showed
that everything that exists is the result of a
constant evolution from cause to effect, and
every effect in turn is a cause, and so on in
one endless chain.

No man ever lived who was not the union
of two forces of opposite polarities, and each

of the forces had a like origin. But more of
this later.

Now, I come to the second, and great twin
discovery to that of Darwin in this nineteenth
century, and it settles the argument advanced
by the Materialist as to the soul ending at
death. It is this: *No human soul ever had a
beginning.*

"Beginnings" have been the great stock in
trade of the church and of various holy books
in all past time. In the "beginning" God
made the heavens and the earth. In the "beginning" God made man out of the dust of the
earth. In the "beginning" the gods of all nations were wont to do wonderful things, and
then modestly step back and allow Nature to
take her course.

Modern astronomers, with the Nebular hy-
pothesis, have upset the "beginning of the
earth." Darwin upset the "beginning" of
man. Now, modern thinkers have at last discovered the fact underlying all Nature, that the
physical universe has its exact counterpart in
the spiritual or astral universe, and that like
laws govern both. Under this great law, we

find that the soul of man is an evolution.

The difference between a man's body and that of a jelly-fish is one of differentiation and advancement towards a higher form. Between a jelly-fish and a squash lies a greater gap of evolution. Between the squash and a boulder lies a still greater gap. Between the boulder and the gas that condensed to make this world lies another wide gap; and yet the fulness of eternal time has been amply sufficient to bring about all these changes and fill all these gaps with an endless chain of cause and effect.

Do not make the mistake of thinking that I claim that the stone became a squash, or the squash a jelly-fish, or the fish a man. The place where each of these forms of matter differentiated or branched off from the main line of descent was far, far back of each.

Thus man no more developed from a horse or an elephant than did an elephant from a man. Each form represents a long line of evolution, extending back far into the great geological epochs of the past history of our planet. We have now arrived at the point where I propose to lay down the great underlying principles of life or intelligence.

As a starter, we must have some place where we pick up this endless chain of evolution, and, ·taking a link for our place of beginning, examine the following links one by one:

1. Matter, and by matter I mean the primordial atoms, always existed, and always will exist. They are uncreated and uncreatable, indestructible and unchangeable.

2. Spirit, and by spirit I mean the primordial vibration peculiar to each kind of atoms, always existed, and always will exist.

In its simplest form, this spirit or astral body is simply inactive in each atom, except as to its own individual vibration; but the instant the physical atom comes into the presence of another atom whose soul vibrates in harmony with its own, attaction is manifested, and the negative pole of one atom is drawn to the positive pole of the other, and a union is the result. This union gives rise to vibratory force, and vibratory force is what we think with and hear with and see with, and smell, taste. love. hate and cognize the universe with.

So you see, my friends, that we have a little

soul born here from two other little father and mother souls. We will say Mr. Oxygen and Miss Hydrogen have been parties to this union,

You must now understand that force never dies. When once generated, it goes on forever. It can be, and is constantly transformed, but it goes on forever, changing and ever changing, according to its environments. When the primordial elements existed, widely separated in space, constituting the immense ball of gas which was to eventually become our earth and her moon, there was no union between the atoms; no birth of souls. The atoms acted under the force of gravity, but their "soul-force" had not been brought in play yet, and no intelligence or vibratory power existed.

As they came nearer and nearer to each other they sought their affinities, and each after its own kind gave birth to souls. But how low down in the scale of creation were those souls? We, in our present high state of development, can scarcely conceive of intelligence so low as these first forms. But still this little was a spark from the Infinite Intelligence. The intelligence manifested in a vegetable is almost inconceivably greater than that in the atoms.

Yet we can hardly cognize even that. When the creeper reaches out for a limb to cling to or the tree brightens up at the fall of rain, we call it "plant instinct." But what of that? When a dog tracks his master through a crowd of men, or a horse pulls the pin out of the gate-post with his teeth, in order to open the gate and pass through, we call that "instinct." That is the vanity of men, and nothing else. I believe that the tree, the oyster and the horse, all have reason, each according to development in the scale of life.

When this conglomeration of atoms I spoke of condensed and combined to form a world, all the potencies and powers existed therein which were destined to form and people that world The germ existed there of every human soul that has ever graduated from this planet, or ever will graduate from it.

Combinations of atoms formed molecules, and these molecules, uniting, formed compounds of higher differentiation, and each combination in turn became disorganized and its ultimates went to form other combinations, and all this time the elemental soul kept pace with the changes, gaining more experience, or soul force at each change, to a higher development. This astral force, having the quality of gradually becoming more intelligent, retains these experiences and becomes more individualized.

To be sure this intelligence is very low at this early stage, as it is but a higher rate of vibration, but this very increase of vibration enables the embryonic soul to embrace a still higher organism at the death of the old one. Thus this reincarnation of soul-force goes on, step by step, through long ages and periods of time. "From the single cell up to man, the life-force has been gaining intelligence by its contact and control of matter; it has aggregated to itself many life-forces to produce one higher, containing the life-principle, the intelligence, the directing matter of the many."

[*W. W. Wheeler, in "Life."*]

This soul-force, as it leaves one body at its dissolution, immediately combines with another, where the union is just being formed. That is, two bodies, each with its own soul-force—combines to form a third, and the liberated astral, finding a suitable abiding place, takes possession. But you must remember that in this chemical union more or less of the old combinations are decompcsed in the change, so that a great part of the force is liberated, to seek other homes.

Chemists are constantly taking advantage of this law of life without knowing really what it is. For instance, I wish to form a certain compound that requires a peculiar astral body, or soul-force, to make it what s required What must I do? I must take steps to liberate the right kind of an astral force at the exact instant that I wish the union to take place. I then get the chemical properties wanted; otherwise I would not.

The reason for this is, that the peculiar astral, having the vibrating force needed, is not common, and under other circumstances than those named, I cannot cause the incarnation. Materialistic chemists explain this property of matter by calling it the *"nascent"* or "just-born state" of matter, which does not explain it at all.

In the formations of some high combina-

tions, chemists are obliged to work up step
by step from lower forms to higher. In other
words, they come to nature's aid and help her
to "create a soul" by a species of rapid evolution, that enables her to turn out in a few
hours an astral body that would, perhaps not
form in ten million years in the ordinary
slow progression of nature, when unaided by
man's intelligence. This is the grand triumph of mind over matter.

In this way our chemists have, by acting
and working under the strict mathematical
laws of the Infinite, formed hundreds of important products. I have here one of them;
it is red aniline a substance which has been
built up synthetically from substances having
a very low soul-force to one that in its highest or crystallized form actually vibrates with
the enormous number of five hundred and
seventy-seven trillions of vibrations per
second, a number so great as to fairly paralyze the understanding.

But let us break up these beautiful green
crystals and note the result. I drop a little
spirits of wine on to them, and lo! what an

instantaneous change. The vibrations are reduced to 471 trillions per second, and you note the change of color to a brilliant red as the vibrations reach your eyes.

You understand, from what I have said, that in all these lower forms the astral does not remain out, but rushes immediately to a new control of matter. Matter gives it the highest expression it has ever known, and it therefore rushes to the nearest union of matter, and supplies the soul-force.

If it would not extend this lecture to too great a length, I would like to tell you of other wonders connected with this "soul of matter." I would tell you of the wonders of chemical affinity, and how substances of widely different qualities are composed of precisely the same elements and in the same proportions.

This shows that just as the soul or astral in a man is what "makes the man," so the astral in an inorganic compound is what gives character to the compound. I would also show you how this soul can be driven out of some substances and made to go long distances before finding its soul-mate, and how

man has ingeniously contrived to use this
force to convey intelligence to distant points.

But to hasten onward over this long road.
The next higher plane of development takes
us into the organic world, into the lower or
vegetable kingdom. The mineral developes
into the vegetable by such slow gradation
that the point where the former leaves off
cannot be detected. But how much more
complex are the chemical combinations, and
how much more unstable. What infinite
variety we find in this kingdom; so great that
a large book could be written upon the soul
of plants. In fact, a book has been written,
entitled, "Evidence of Intelligence in the
Vegetable World."

For millions of years this kingdom held
full sway upon the earth, while the physical
development and the astral, went on hand in
hand, from the lowest forms of life to the
highest. There is as much, if not more, difference between the soul of a toadstool and
that of a plant called "fly-catcher" as there
is between the soul of an oyster and that of
a horse. But there is so little difference

between some forms of vegetable life and the lowest forms of animal life that it has been a mooted question as to which kingdom some of them belong.

As soon though as we are fairly across the boundary line we begin to detect the evidence of a higher intelligence, a greater soul-development. We soon arrive at animals capable of moving about and seeking their food, and even "thinking," so far as to take good care of themselves, They are "progressive thinkers," too, for the soul-developement goes on, ever onward, re-incarnating from one form to another, never remaining separated from matter any length of time, except under certain unusual conditions, until in the course of ages we find them advanced to the lower forms of humanity.

We will leave them there for the **present**, and in a subsequent lecture take them **up** and follow the soul of man upward from its lower forms, step by step, even into the life beyond, and even higher, as it struggles on toward the INFINITE.

The Soul of Man.

THE ADVANCEMENT OF MAN TOWARD THE HIGHER LIFE AND OUR DUTIES IN THIS ADVANCEMENT.

DEVELOPMENT OF THE SOUL — OUR EARTHLY SCHOOL — THE DARK AGES — INFLUENCE OF THE ASTRAL OVER THE MENTAL — "EXCEPT YE BE BORN AGAIN" — A NEW CYCLE OF ETERNITY — EACH SOUL A VIBRATING INTELLECTUAL ENTITY — ONWARD AND UPWARD.

ONE of my former lectures treated of the astral body or soul of man, as being an evolution like the physical body, and traced the soul force upward from the vibrations of primordial atoms, from one incarnation to another, through the mineral vegetable and animal worlds to man. I pro-

pose to begin where I then left off and take
the soul where it first became baptized with
the light of intelligence which divides the
human soul from that of the lower animal.

Now, my friends, do not make the mistake
of thinking there was a line of demarcation
between this newly enlightened soul and the
one from which it originated or sprang.   Not
at all.   The first little dawn of humanity was
so very slight an improvement upon that immediately preceding it, that an observer could
not h ·· noticed, probably, any difference; yet
there v·s a difference.   That soul had come
back n any, many times, and had received
much of earthly experience by incarnating
under more and more favorable conditions, until it had arrived at a state where it could grasp
some thought that it was unable to grasp
before.

But when the time was, that the God of
Reason said: "Let there be light." we know
not. We only know from reasoning it out, that
it was hundreds of thousands of years ago   Man
had progressed for many thousands of years
before he arrived at the stage of astral develop-

ment of which we see evidences in the stone
age, when he carried on wars, hunted wild
beasts, and made exquisite arrow heads from
flint stones. The skulls found in mounds and
caves, belonging to that age, show by their
frontal development only a slight difference in
intellectual power between them and modern
skulls.

In other words, the human soul has developed only enough in ten thousand years to
require an addition of seven-eighths of an inch
to the size of its house or headquarters.

Remember another thing also. Unhappily
this progression is not constant. The old earth
has had its ups and downs, and as environments
have changed, so the astral man has had his
ups and downs, sometimes retrograding for
manycenturies, then advancing for a period of
time which in some cases was short and in
others long.

Thus, we have been thousands on thousands
of years regaining the place in spiritual growth
and God-like knowledge which we lost when
the grand old kingdom of Atlantis sank beneath
the waves and left Egypt to take her place.

In order that the astral body or soul may
continue to advance, it must constantly find
better and better conditions to which it can
come at its various incarnations; like a school
boy, who starts in the lowest grade of our city
school, and year by year comes back after each
vacation to a higher grade, and thus continues
to advance. Let the boy come back to a poorer
and lower school than the one last attended, and
he ceases to advance.

This teaches the important fact that we
should do all we can to make this school better.
Yes, my friends, we all have a personal interest
in keeping up the standard of intelligence in
this earthly school. so that when we return
after our vacation, more or less protracted, we
may be enabled to advance in knowledge, light,
power, love and spiritual growth, and thus take
a new step upward, instead of one downward.

Think, dear friends, of the prospect for advancement found by any of the souls here to-
night, who came back to this earth during the
Dark Ages, which lasted twelve hundred and
sixty years.

Think of an enlightened astral of old Atlantis coming back here during that soul-blighting time, times and half a time, the dark and terrible "forty and two months" of ancient prophecy, during which the spirit of God was trampled to the earth and the dark and damnable creeds of men reigned and made slaves of the people.

But, thank heaven, we now live in an age of progression. Never before in history has there been a time when so many unselfish souls, upon either shore, were working together for the great end we have in view,—the advancement of mankind. You, who are within the fold, understand the importance of this grand work. You understand the great advancement that has already taken place, and many millions outside this Temple understand it, through the great wave of psychic power that has swept the earth from the four quarters thereof, even to the innermost parts.

The trumpet of the angel is sounding. Let those who have ears to hear, listen to it. See that ye have not the mark of the beast in your hands or your foreheads. See that your hearts are pure in the sight of the Lord of Light and Love.

The question is often asked of us: "If the astral, or soul of man, has lived in other bodies, why is it that we have no memory of it in our present state of existance?" For the same reason that a sleep-walker has no memory, when awakened, of what he thought, said and did while in the somnambulistic state. He may have composed abeautiful poem, or, on the other hand he may have taken a pleasant moonlight stroll upon the parapet of a four story building; in either case he has acted from the knowledge possessed by that "inner man," and when he comes back to the use of his present faculties, he knows naught of what has occurred. An impassable bar has been erected between the astral and the mental.

A wise provision it is that this is so. Let a child come into the world with all the accumulated knowledge of a sage at his command, and see how awkward it would be. He would not improve himself in wisdom and knowledge. He would simply use the vast store he already possessed to the detriment, perhaps, of his fellow-mortals.

But while the sensor nerves of man do not

communicate to the presiding spirit in man the knowledge, memories, etc., appertaining to the astral part of the soul combination, it is a fact that the presence and power of the astral is constantly felt by the mind and senses.

Thus it is that many persons have longings for something they hardly know what — flashes of memories of grand and beautiful things that they cannot understand. One lady feels as if she had seen herself sweeping grandly through the lofty halls of a palace, dressed in robes of silk, woven with pearls; but in this life she has had no such experience.

All is explained when we find that this flash of feeling and thought is communicated from an astral soul that once occupied the body of a queen of Egypt, and has preserved the memory through all subsequent incarnations.

No person has or can have the true mystic knowledge which alone enables one to grasp the great truths of life and the mysteries of the Omnipotent, unless he or she has enjoyed advantages in past incarnations which have raised the soul to the higher plane of knowledge. Souls who have not advanced to this place can only grasp a very little here at this incarnation. But I assure you that even that little is a starter. One little step has been taken upon the right road, and it will be followed by others in due time.

The soul that holds the slate in one incarnation, performs the mathematical work of a master in the next. The soul that is driven from its habitation in one incarnation, because it concocts a work directed against priestcraft and creeds, comes among us again and, under the inspiration communicated to a new mind in this age, publishes a periodical that scourges with whips of fire the very powers that once persecuted him, and publishes their shame over a continent.

It is said: "The mills of the gods grind slowly, but exceeding fine." A good illustration of a great truth in nature it is. The wicked triumph for a time, but not forever. Fate will overtake them in due time. He that vainly thinks that because he rides in his carriage and commands great riches or power now, he will have a fine place in the next life, reckons without his host. He will find he has not laid up the treasures of knowledge in heaven, where none can steal; but riches upon earth, where his heirs will quarrel over them perhaps.

We do not advocate the eating of skim milk here, in the expectation of having cream in the next world, as Col. Ingersoll so aptly puts it; but on the contrary, we believe in making use of all honorable means of rational enjoyment. Dress well and live well as your means will permit. Sisters, think not that you will offend the Infinite if you wear the jewels that you love or the beautiful dress that enhances your beauty. On every side we see the beautiful flowers, the magnificient plumage of birds and a thousand varied tints that go to make up lovely nature.

Why should our highest and best creation of all depart from this rule of God, and hide their charms in black, ungainly gowns and poke bonnets? Ask those poor things whom you meet upon the street, with pallid faces and bands of white from forehead to chin, how they dare to thus fly in the face of God's holy law of being? Oh! woe! woe unto the wretches who have deluded them into throwing away the bright promise of womanhood; into selling their birthright for a mess of pottage.

God help the poor souls who become lost to all eternity; yes, literally lost in a never-ending hell—the hell of ignorance! Lost through a lack of a true knowledge of the universe! Lost forever, through missing the means of salvation by purification of soul, by reincarnation under the best conditions.

What said a master of old? "Except ye are born again, ye cannot enter the kingdom of heaven." Did he know what he was talking about? My dear friends, he did. He also meant just what he said. He did not mean by a "new birth" the joining one's self to a Methodist church or a Baptist church or the Salvation Army. Nothing of the kind. He knew from the inner light possessed by him that man must be born again and again before he can arrive at the point where he can enter the narrow gate and enjoy the mansions on high, not made with hands, eternal in the heavens.

In our Father's mansion there are many houses. From the shining balance of the se-

cret portal to the Temple of Wisdom upon the
right-hand side of honor and glory stretches a
long road, from house to house, and few there
are that are able to climb the hill of knowledge
o'er the rough and rugged way.

When I think of the vast work we have before us, a work no less than the regeneration
of a world, no less than providing the means
that will enable millions yet unborn to see the
glorious light; I say when I think of this and
look about me at the faithful little band of
workers gathered here in this great city that
stands over the ashes of ancient Bab, and
think how small we are, and how great is the
work, my heart nearly fails me.

But, friends, we are not alone. Millions
of bright sons and daughters of the light
stand ready to help us. Bright beings, who
are angles of love to a waiting world, stretch
forth their hands to us, and beckon us onward and upward in the star-strewn path of
light. On every hand recruits are pressing
towards our standard. The little rock that
fell upon the toes of the image a few years
ago will soon cover the feet of iron and clay.

Perhaps I have wandered far from my subject. I should have traced man's soul upward perhaps, through all these ages past and gone, through all his struggles for light. I should have shown the life that awaits us in the astral universe, and how we live and learn and have our being under those strange conditions. But could I do this? Could I unfold these things before the gaze of the outer world without touching upon things that we are sworn to hold sacred and secret?

But this I can say: Man's astral body is a work of his environments during all the time that has passed. Its future growth will come from all environments to come. But the time when the period of greatest development takes place, is from the time thinking and reasoning men developed upon this earth, up to the period when the earth will become too cold to give conditions of favorable life. The length of time which any given planet furnishes these good conditions, depends upon the size of the globe, its density and distance from the sun around which it revolves.

As far as we know, no two planets ever

existed with precisely the same conditions. While many worlds are far ahead of ours in an opportunity for their inhabitants to become highly developed, on the other hand there are a far greater number that do not possess our advantages.

We must take advantage of our condition to make all of ourselves that is possible, for, when the school closes, it will never open for us again. We have passed through to our graduation, and our diplomas show our rank. We must take our place in the great hereafter, and progress as best we may, for our earthly race is run.

When millions and millions of years have passed and a new cycle of eternity produces conditions that causes this earth of ours to melt with fervent heat and the firmament to pass away as a scroll, then a new heaven and a new earth will appear, but not for us. Our heaven will become grander and higher when that time comes. We will have no attraction to that new earth; it will belong to others. The school is closed to us and we are what we have made ourselves, no more, no less.

Each soul is an intellectual entity, unlike any other in all the universe, a vibrating force unto itself. If a soul possesses the necessary qualifications for being happy the universe is a home of love, a heaven. If a soul has, through ignorance, cultivated bad qualities, such as envy, jealousy and hate, such a soul finds its level, and finds a hell wherever it goes.

Therefore, my dear ones, I charge you to cultivate only the best. Cultivate honesty, purity,, sobriety and kind feeling toward each other, and all mankind, if possible. Seek to love your neighbor as yourselves. Throw no obstacle in the way of another. Cultivate a loving and philanthropical charity to all mankind.

Try to bear ever in mind the great law of life, that you cannot rise by the downfall of another. In seeking to pull others downward you lower yourselves.

Endeavor to uplift your fellows, and thereby advance yourselves, step by step, from one mystic circle of light to another, adding star after star to your crown of glory as you rise upward, onward, towards INFINITY.

LECTURE VIII.

8 - 2-4-23

Differentiation.

ASTRAL FORCE AND MAGNETIC VIBRATION.

MAGNETIC DIFFERENTIATION IN PLANTS — POLAR ANGLES OF EARTH—THE "RISING SIGN "—EXACTNESS IN ASTRAL LAWS AND CALCULATIONS — DIFFERENTIATION BY ROCKS, PLANTS AND TREES, FROM LOW TO HIGH — ZODIACAL DIFFERENTIATION IN MAN - WOMAN AS THE CROWNING GLORY OF EARTH, LIFE, ETC.

SOME of my former lectures have set forth my theories relative to astral magnetism, showing how it proceeds from all bodies in the universe according to their several chemical constitutions, and how the effect is transmitted by means of vibration, in the wonderful substance called " Ether,' which prevades all space and all matter equally. This evening I intend to go a step farther and show you how these magnetic vibrations affect plants and animals in general and parts of animals and some plants specifically in their various parts. Not that vegetable and animal life are exceptions in this respect, as the very earth itself, formed as it is of inorganic matter, receives these vibratory forces, and responds to them, with different degrees of impressibility according to the latitude and longitude of a particular part.

This property of the earth has been spoken of in all ancient works on astrology as the "ruling sign" of a given country, or the "rising sign" of a person or place, which is equivalent to saying: " The polar angle of the earth at such a place is equal to such a sign." No attempt has ever been made to explain these obscure terms, but, on the contrary, the whole science of Solar Biology and Astral Delineation has been rendered so obscure by the terms used as to make it little better than a happy-go-lucky piece of guess work.

Happily for the good of the science, modern mathematicians and astronomers are not satisfied with guess work or approximate results, as were those of the middle ages. The common people even, demand exactness in scientific reasoning and conclusions. This demand must be filled.

There is a law throughout nature, that the higher a body is developed the more it has the power of differentiating the planetary effects, or the magnetic vibrations. Thus, a stone is of a very low development, and consequently receives all the vibrations in a body without differentiation as to any part of its body; but a plant or tree is higher in the scale, therefore it differentiates the astral vibrations in some cases into four parts, corresponding to four quarters of the Zodiac. All plants do not have this power to such an extent, however. While one plant differentiates as to its root, bark, berry and leaf, another only receives in the leaf and root differently.

The higher we go in the scale of development the more this characteristic increases, until we arrive at the crowning glory of earthly life, woman! Now brothers do not be shocked. You know I am an iconoclast, and my bump of reverence is small, so forgive me if I set aside the cherished doctrines of bygone ages and assert that woman, not man, is the higher development. Shall I tell you why?

There are several facts which support this conclusion. But saying nothing of the physiological development of the female, which is differentiated higher to fit the requirements of generation and her functions in life; saying nothing of her fineness of structure and capability of withstanding suffering that her brother would fall under; saying nothing of all of this, there is one little fact that alone supports the theory. It is this: The more perfectly the spiritual or astral body balances the physical body, the higher is the development. A stone has a strong physical body, with the very lowest astral body to balance it. A tree has a higher physical body, with a higher astral than has the rock.

Following up in the scale, we find that the female of the human species has a higher spiritual development to balance the physical than has the male. She is more intuitive, which is really "seeing with spiritual eyes." More mediumistic and more clairvoyant.

Remember, I am only speaking as a general
rule; there are exceptions on both sides, of
course. These facts are my excuse for calling your attention to this chart, which

exhibits a female form with the signs of
the Zodiac in the order of nature, running from

Aries the Ram, around to the right in regular order as moves the earth in its orbit about the sun, to Pisces on the left. From a spiritual point of view the signs begin at Libra, over the head of the woman, and decend to her feet, rising upon her right. This signification will be readily understood by members of the Order who have been duly "weighed in the balance" and not found wanting.

But when we come to the specific effects of the astral vibrations, corresponding to the twelve houses or signs of the Zodiac, we find a different arrangement necessary in order to indicate the parts of the form ruled by each sign. The chart on page 122 shows the change from former position

There we find the signs arranged from Aries at the head, running down the body as indicated by the pointers to Pisces at the feet. The parts indicated in the chart, correspond to, or are said to be "ruled by the house" as marked. The meaning of this is, that man has developed so highly as to be differentiated to twelve places of vibration, the highest of all earthly creations.

Think of the vast change that has taken place in the human astral or soul since the time when the entire soul-force consisted of the slight magnetic attraction of the positive

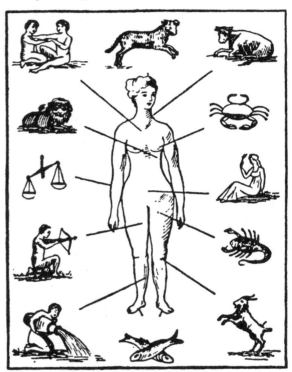

and negative poles of two insignificant monads of a palaeozoic sea. For such is the start of a human soul on all earths and planets. These inhabitable globes are all nurseries of astral forms that must, through the inherent laws of being keep progressing on and ever onward, from the scarcely to be recognized soul of the lowest dual form of life to be seen under our most powerful microscopes.

Nature never stands still for a moment. All, all, is one vast moving, evoluting, vibrating mass. Man can differentiate to but one more place in the physical body. He covers the twelve Zodiacal signs now - the center is to come. The center is the sun. Friends, you must become sons and daughters of LIGHT; become possessed of the thirteenth power, and when enough of the inhabitants of the earth have differentiated to that point, we have the long sought for millennium. I am assured that it will come, and is in fact dawning upon us to-day. But in the mean time we must deal with men and women as we find them now.

THE TWELVE SIGNS OF THE ZODIAC.

Affect the various portions of the body according to the polarity of the earth at the twelve points marked by the twelve houses. Between these polarities there are points and shades of all degrees of magnetic force or vibration, corresponding to the motion of the earth during certain times. These are graded down so fine that we have even the logarithms of minutes and seconds, the latter however, being computed to five seconds variation of differential time. This fineness of computation in our tables of astral force, is what enables masters of heliocentric astronomy to perform feats that were utterly impossible before these laws were formulated.

It was by means of these tables of astral logarithms that the great law was discovered and formulated that plants and all vegetable productions are ruled by the law of vibration. and each plant, root, bark, herb, leaf, wood, bud, nut or berry used in medical practice, owes. its power to its rate and ratio of magnetic vibration.

EACH PLANET RULES A PLANT

in each of the houses of the Zodiac: and some planets rule many vegetable productions in each house. These plants produce effects upon the human economy, when taken as medicine corresponding to the combined vibratory effects of the sign and the planet that rules the plant.

Thus we find from observations recorded during many centuries, that plants partake of the characteristics of the planets they are ruled by. For an illustration of this law take

THE RULINGS OF ARIES.

Mercury rules Cascarilla.
Venus   "   Nutmeg.
Mars   "   Canabis Indica
Jupiter   "   Eucalyptus
Saturn   "   Aconite
Uranus   "   Thyme
Neptune   "   Angelica

You will notice in this table of rulings, that Saturn, the planet of sickness and death, rules Aconite, the deadly plant called "Monkshood,' while Venus, the planet of life, health, and love, rules nutmeg, a thing that has simply exhilarating tonic qualities. But we find that every one of these seven articles under Aries, set up vibrations in the human system affecting the head and the circulation generally. The head is the "headquarters," so to speak, of fevers, although symptoms may manifest themselves in all parts of the system. Thus we notice symptoms indicating disease ruling under Aries to be—flushed face, thirst, dry tongue, hot forehead and temples, rapid pulse, dry skin, etc. But this effect soon sets up bad effects at the opposite pole, and cold feet, trembling limbs, aching knees, tc., often follow, or co-ordinate therewith.

Now what is needed to restore the normal vibration so that the system of the poor fever-stricken patient can respond to the health giving magnetism of Venus and her co-ordinating planets?

Shall we poison the system with Dovers Powder in large doses, one ingredient of which rules in Leo (opium), another in Gemini (Ipecac), or shall we select Aconite alone, the ruler under Saturn in Aries, and dose the patient with that until the over vibrations set up such a state that it takes an entire quadrature of Mercury, 21 days, for the patient to recover. That used to be the practice in old times, those "good old times" we read of, when nearly every one expected to have a "run of fever" every spring, as much as they expected to see grass grow. Our friends of the Homeopathic

School of medicine have long seen the fallacy
of this style of medication and have made
elaborate catalogues of symptoms caused by
these over vibrations set up by the various
drugs and medicines of the pharmacopœia.
They have done a noble work, a grand work.
They have saved the lives of millions; but the
one weak spot in their system, is the uncertainty
of the action of the remedy in such attenuated
doses. Of course I must admit, that some
physicians of that school cure cases with what
they call "high potencies." I have had a physician gravely tell me that he cured a case of
erupting pimples, with the hair falling off
and a dirty pallid complexion, with a few days
treatment of a dose each day of *Natrum
Muriaticum* at the one thousanth potency.
To an unprofessional person, this sounds like
a pretty strong treatment, especially when
the term "potency" is used; but, to one who
understands that Natrum Muriaticum is simply common table salt, an article that we are
full of all the time from top to toe, and that
the thousanth potency means that one grain
of salt has been triturated until it is diluted

with more than ten thousand tons of sugar of milk, and then a grain of that trituration, diluted with a million tons more of sugar of milk. I say to a person who knows this fact (and it is below the truth as to quantity) it seems prepost rous. Yet, the stubborn fact remains that the physician spoke the truth when he said he made the cure, and I have no doubt that thousands of such cases are on record.

Now I will give my theory of this and all are welcome to take it or leave it as they feel inclined. I firmly believe, that when cures are affected through high potency homeopathic remedies, such cures are performed by the magnetism of the physician himself, unconsciously going with the medicine. When the physician prescribes them himself they do the work required of them, but let a person try to doctor himself with the same high dilution, and he will generally fail. Do not understand me as saying that homeopathic remedies have no effect, for I do not mean it. In fact I know the contrary. If my theories of medicine are correct, the homeopathic idea of *semilia similibus curantur* is the true theory and is on the right road; only in practice it has not been carried far enough in one direction, and too far in another. I mean by this, that differentiation of remedies and their combination according to vibratory effect, in one homogeneous mixture, has not been attempted by homeopathists with success as yet; while on the other hand, the dilution of simple remedies has been carried too far for general use.

Remember now, that I am saying nothing against homeopathy as a science, and do not deny that the medicines have powerful effects; nor do I dispute the law of *similia*; I only believe that many carry it too far and that single plant remedies stop short of the best and greatest good obtainable.

"*Between two extremes lies wisdom,*" said an ancient philosopher, and I think that in the case of medical practice, that between the single remedy and attenuated doses of homeopathy upon one hand and the heroic and exterminating doses of allopathy on the

other, lies the true science of medicine. With
our present light on the subject, it seems to
me that combinations of the active principals
of the seven planets ruling in each sign and
affecting the human system as illustrated in
the above diagram, comes as near to a scientific theory of medicine as is possible.

The subject of medicine may seem dry to
some of you, yet it is one of great importance.
You have learned in this Temple that every
thing is governed by the same Divine Laws.
That the insignificant grain of sand obeys the
same inexorable laws as does the giant Jupiter, who, with his own bulk, eighty-eight
thousand miles in diameter, and his retinue
of four large satellites, pursues his spiral path
through the mighty void of space at the rate
of four hundred and seventy-five miles per
minute, and at the same time, obeying the
tremendous power of attraction, following
our sun upon his enormous pathway among
the stars at the rate of over one thousand
miles per minute.

Nothing is too small or too large for us to
learn a lesson from. The little animalcule

that lives within the holes and caves of the grain of sand, regards his home as a great world. We, who live upon this planet, earth, regard it as a giant globe; but my friends, the eyes of science look beyond mere appearances, and see that this earth, with all her sister planets, with our vast sun and all the satellites, comets and meteoric streams of matter belonging to our solar system, covering a space in the heavenly void more than five billion miles in extent, is, after all, but a grain of sand on the shores of eternity, compared with what is even within the ken of the telescopes used by men.

I might even say that the entire cluster of suns, over sixteen millions in number, which constitutes our siderial system and form a vast whirling mass of suns and planets, with all its stupendous magnitude, is nothing but a drop, a speck, a grain of matter in the great ocean of INFINITY.

LECTURE IX.

Evolution of Matter.

PEEDING ever onward through infinite space, at a mean distance of about twenty trillions of miles from his nearest neighbor suns, our sun holds sway over a little band of planets, asteroids, comets, and meteors, which seemingly obey his will and perform their revolutions in many elliptical orbits, of more or less elongation about him.

Our sun is a body eight hundred and

fifty thousand miles in diameter, as large as
twelve hundred and forty-five thousands of
earths rolled into one, with a mass over six
hundred times greater than all of his subordin-
ates together, and a gross weight of nearly
two octillions of tons. Such is the vast power
of gravitation possessed by this mass of matter
that the center of gravity of the entire system
is within the body of the sun. Properly and
scientifically speaking, no body in the universe
revolves about another. Each combination, or
cluster of bodies, revolves about the center of
gravity of the cluster, subject to slight per-
turbations from other more remote clusters
and masses of matter. Another thing should
be understood, and that is that although from
a theoretical and mathematical standpoint all
sorts of heavenly bodies move in circles and
elliptical orbits, as a matter of absolute fact
not a single body moves in the form and
manner theoretically determined.

EXPLANATION OF THIS FACT.

Take the moon, for instance. In theory it
revolves about the earth, but must we consider that while the moon is performing its

revolution in twenty-seven and one-third days, the earth is constantly moving forward in its revolution about the sun at a velocity of about eighteen miles per second, or a total distance during the lunar circuit of nearly forty-six millions of miles.

The effect of this motion is to cause the moon's real path to become a simple wave-like motion, curving in and out like the path of a snake; but this is not all, for in addition to this the earth, while theoretically performing its revolution about the sun in one year, is, in reality, only forming a long spiral curve drawn out to conform to a motion of our sun, forward in his orbit over five-hundred millions of miles. The effect of this motion is to still further complicate the motion of the moon.

But this is only a beginning, for the entire cluster to which our sun belongs is moving through space at an immense velocity about the center of gravity of the nebulæ to which it belongs, and still we have another motion of the entire nebulæ about some other far-off center, and so on to Infinity.

So the entire effect of all this complicated

system of motions is to cause the real path of our moon to be nearer to a straight line through space than to anything else.

In fact a prominent master has made a curious calculation, showing that not only our moon and earth, but all the heavenly bodies are actually moving in lines straighter than men with the finest instruments could lay off. He demonstrated that with only the elements of the motions of the three bodies, sun, earth and moon taken into consideration in the calculation, that the moon only varied from a perfectly straight path one 200th part of a hair's breadth to the mile.

Man never could and never will construct so straight a line as that. Now add to this all these greater uncalculated motions beyond, and what man can say but that the little fraction of a hair's breadth itself may be wiped out.

What is true of one is true of all. Among infinities each and every calculation results in the same. The law that applies to our little moon, applies to our sun and all suns in the same general terms, because in both cases we carry the calculation of motion to infinity. For instance, let us illustrate: Let the variation of the moon from a right line equal x. Let the variation of the earth equal y.

We must theoretically assume that x is the greater, because a satellite has a greater variation than his primary.

Now let $x - y = d$, the difference between the variations, and we can readily see that d becomes less and less as our calculations embrace more and more cycles of motion. Carry the process of reduction to infinity and d is reduced to zero. So we conclude that all bodies in space are in rapid motion, in practically straight, or at least in very different lines than those found by considering only one or two links in the system.

But we give this more as a matter of curiosity or speculation than anything else, for we are well aware that we must mathmematically consider each heavenly body as if moving about a fixed center. This center may not contain any body whatever. For instance let O—— P— -O represent two-bodies of equal gravatic force belonging to a system, and there are many such cases in the universe, and each will revolve about the point P, half way between the two bodies, although there is no matter there to attract.

This great law of equilibrium of forces and mutual attraction between masses of matter, disposes of the theory that there must be a great central sun around which all revolve. Such a thing would be really an impossibility, inasmuch as we cannot conceive of a center to a thing that has no circumference, and most certainly space can have no limits or circumscribing lines.

There are two great forces in nature that are constantly acting together in the production and evolution of suns and worlds, and all that exists.

Acting in concert and harmonizing throughout all the works of Nature these two great forces are amply sufficient to produce, transform and recreate all forms of existances either spiritual or material.

Both of these forces belong to the great ONE force, but occupy different ends of the great "Celestial Spectrum" or universal magnet.

The two great forces can again be subdivided thus:

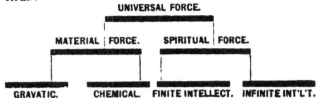

Each end of this celestial magnet has common properties. Thus gravatic force acts at long distances without limit, while chemical force acts at short range and is thus limited. On the spirit side the Infinite Intelligence acts at long distance and is without limit, while the finite intelligence is limited to the short range of experience.

A perfect balance is, therefore, constant between the material and spiritual forces. This duality can be noticed all through the range of matter and spirit, with the same wonderful likeness existing between the two grand forces.

For instance, the force of gravity brings matter into nearer relations, so that its co-ordinate force, chemical, can act and thus unite atoms of matter in more harmony and union. On the other end of the magnet Infinite Intelligence constantly acts in such a way as to bring intelligence into closer relations, so that its co-ordinate, finite intelligence, can come in play and unite and increase in power.

I have been most forcibly struck, upon many occasions, with the action of certain chemicals, under manipulation and combination. They seemed to have such likes and dislikes for each other, that some of them impressed me as almost having reason. In fact, I have every reason to believe that there is a low form of vibratory force, that might be denominated the first glimmerings of reason or soul force.

No man can limit the Infinite and say "we understand it all."

There are many rates of vibration in all departments of physics that cannot be cognized by man's limited senses. A few octaves of sound, as air vibrations; a few octaves of light, as etheric vibrations; a few octaves of magnetism, or odyllic vibrations; a few octaves of intelligence, or psychic vibrations, are all man can compass while confined within the environments of the flesh.

All nature might be likened to a vast magnet, with the spiritual at one end and the material at the other:

Matter.	N	Spirit.
A B C D E	F G	H I K

N is the neutral point, or place where the two grand divisions meet. Every substance in the universe takes its place along the length of this magnet, according to its rate of vibration and density of material. The more density and less vibration of atoms possessed by anything, the nearer it comes to the material end.

The same substance may have its atoms driven further apart and at the same time the rate of its vibrations increased, so as to change its place upon the magnet.

Illustration: Take ice, which is the natural state of water in the absence of heat. Say it ranges in the magnet at B. Raise its rate of vibration by means of heat and the liquid and mobile article water is formed, standing, say at C. Apply a higher vibration of chaloric and steam results. This body is invisible to our eyes, and its atoms are driven much further apart. Its rate of vibration is greatly increased, as may be observed in its pounding force against the sides of its containing vessel. It now ranges at D. Apply still more heat, say the vibrations of red, and we decompose the steam into gas, with a greatly increased vibratory force, while its ultimate atoms are driven widely apart. It ranges at E now. In other words, we have changed its place nearly to the neutral point. The same can be done with iron or steel, or any substance that exists, only some require more vibration to drive the atoms apart than do others. But we can safely assume, and maintain it by the soundest argument, that no matter how high the rate of atomic vibration may be raised, or how far apart the ultimate atoms of a body may be driven, the material is all there. Not one particle can be annihilated. This is an important fact that all should understand, for it is the key that unlocks many mysteries.

Thus, we may understand that the human soul, or spiritualized being, is not a being made of *nothing*, "projected from some great soul center," as some maintain, but it is an absolute entity, composed of highly evoluted, refined and attenuated atoms, with a high rate of vibration far up toward the infinite end of the magnet, say at II.

It is a stange fact that so many entities in the universe must have their rate of vibration either raised or lowered before they become tangible to some one or more of man's physical senses. The reason for this is that there are wide gaps in the "sense spectrum" of man. Between the highest number of vibrations of sound cognizable by his ear, to the lowest number seen by the eye as color or light, stretches a wide gap, only partially filled by octaves here and there, that make themselves manifest to us by being in multiple relations to our sense vibrations.

All this should teach us that to deny a thing because we cannot see it, taste it or hear it, smell or feel it, is as foolish as was the old gentleman in arguing that the world did not "revolve upon its axes," because he set a pail of water upon a stump over night and found it unspilled in the morning.

Let us constantly strive for a better understanding of these great and Divine laws and forces that make and govern the worlds, and we may be perfectly content with the truth and nothing but the truth, for the universe is so grand, so great, so wonderful in all its appointments, when rightly understood, that the most ultra-fanciful theories gotten up by speculative persons, sink into insignificance in comparison, with the grandeur and glory of the Omnipotnt Work.

LECTURE X.

Evolution in General.

KEY TO THE SECRETS OF THE UNIVERSE.

The only Explanation of the Origin of Things.

THE THEORY OF SPECIAL CREATIONS--EVOLUTION OF THE EQUINE RACE—A LOCOMOTIVE OR A SHIP, AN EVOLUTION LANGUAGES AND RELIGIONS EVOLUTE—EVOLUTION THE KEY TO WISDOM.

ONE of the most wonderful things in Nature to me, is that the universal law of evolution is so little understood by the masses. Even educated and otherwise observant persons seem to be thickheaded or obtuse when contemplating this subject.

I cannot understand why such a simple self-evident proposition should be held in any more

doubt than that twice two make four; but I
am compelled to face the fact that there is
room for doubt, just as I am compelled to accept the fact that men and women living in
Chicago to-day, in this enlightened Nineteenth
Century, believe that we are living on the in-
side of a hollow globe, instead of on the outside of an earth, and that day and night are
caused by the sun having one dark side and
one light; or that there are those who claim to
be teachers that hold that the earth is flat like
a pancake.

I am going to try in this address to show, in
the plainest language I can command, why I
think it wonderful that the world cannot understand the subject of evolution.

Now, friends, let us reason calmly and good-
naturedly together.

Did you ever see, upon this earth, anything
that had no antecedents? Did you ever see
a hen's egg that was not laid by a hen? Did
you ever see a hen that was not once a
chicken? Did you ever see a chicken that did
not hatch from an egg? You must answer no
to all these questions.

Thus we find that now, in this age at least, the law holds good that everything comes from some thing or things that immediately preceded it and was the cause of the same. Behind each and every one, are their two parents, as far back as any history extends.

Now, this fact being once established; by what species of reasoning can we assume that laws that are fixed and immutable *now*, as far as human knowledge can take cognizance of anything, were once different, and so entirely different that there could not be any comparison.

For instance: Try to conceive of a world of "Special Creations," for that is what you and every one must conceive of and admit, provided you do not take the evolution view. We will go back to a time when, say a horse was needed. No horse was upon the earth, nor had there been one. All right we will have a horse, or rather a span of them, in order to start the race of equines.

The animal must be made from several elements—oxygen, hydrogen, carbon, nitrogen, phosphorus and many other elementary bodies must be gotten together, some of them combined by processes found going on now only in certain plants and then all must be put together in a wonderful and complex combination of bones, flesh, skin, hair, organs of respiration, digestion, hearing, sight and a hundred other wonderful parts that go to make up that noble animal.

Well, the job is done. Now who set the animal up? Who put him together? How did any being, human, superhuman or divine go to work to do this wonderful thing? When did he or it do it? Why should he do it once and not again? If an infinite God did this, by what means did he bring it about? My friends, stop a moment and consider calmly the absurdity of all this.

It seems to me you cannot help but admit that every animal upon the earth shows in his very formation, and every limb and part, an adaptation of means to ends that could only come through a long series of improvements and slow changes under environments.

Suppose, for a moment, that you should go to some ignorant person and say to him,

"Here is a house standing on this lot, that is very wonderful. It was all made just as it stands. Nothing was used that existed before." Do you suppose you could make him believe you for a moment? No! He would laugh at you or think you crazy; for he, let him be however ignorant, would know that the lumber must have been manufactured from trees that had been years and years growing. That the nails were made of iron that had been smelted and changed from the raw ore by the patient labor of men, and afterwards rolled, hammered and cut. He would know that articles enter into the construction of that building, that have been made as the result of ages of experience and invention.

Thus a house, a ship, or a printing press, is an evolution. The locomotive of to-day could not have been made or invented by mortal man a hundred years ago. It, too, is a work of evolution piece by piece.

Improvement after improvement was added as men gained in experience, until we have the complete structure as it stands to-day, the iron horse that has changed the conditions of human existance.

"But," says one who can only reason upon the surface of things: "I cannot believe that I ever came from a baboon, gorilla or a monkey." My friend, you never did, in all probability. But look back a few hundred years at your ancestors, and see if there has been any change in the stock under the surroundings of civilization.

Have you a better chance than your father had? Did he have a better chance than did his great-great-great grandfather? Did that worthy old progenitor show a speck of improvement upon the ancestors that preceded him a thousand years ago? If so, perhaps you can take your mind back thirty, forty, or fifty thousand years, and come to a time when a flat-headed, strong-jawed ancestor of yours, living in some cave or forest lair, would not have been offended at being told that his great grandfather belonged to that despised race of quadrumana.

But fifty thousand years is too short a time for all these wonderful changes. Why, according to our best evidence, obtained from the study of geology and palæontology, it has taken not less than fifty thousand years to develop the horse from his early form as a small animal with toes, more like a fox of to-day, than like his modern representative. But fifty thousand years is nothing to the time nature took to develop that small prototype from still lower forms of animal life.

In the case of the horse, each and every link has been found in fossiliferous deposits, leading step by step up to the historical period. Friends, has there been any change in that animal during the last twenty-five years? Stop and think. Did your great grandfather ever see a horse trot a mile in two minutes and eleven seconds? Why, no! bless your heart. We used to hurrah ourselves hoarse over a horse that could make a mile in 2:40, not longer than twenty-five years ago.

This is evolution, divested of complicated terms and brought within the understanding of children. Everything evolutes and changes constantly. By this process worlds are formed and peopled. Religions evolute. Languages

evolute. Our very ideas are simply the product of evolution.

Ministers are evoluting from the churches,
because the rank and file cannot keep up with
the thinkers who have nothing else to do but
study.   He leaves his congregation behind.
All kinds of isms and cults are going through
the process of evolution.   Fifty years will
place the orthodox religion where we stand
now; but by that time we will be far on along
the Infinite path, and as far from them as ever.

Evolution is the glorious key to the storehouse of the Infinite.   It unlocks the secrets
of Nature and tells us how all things came to
exist.

LECTURE XI.

𝔏ife 𝔅eginnings.

FROM WHENCE DID LIFE COME TO OUR GLOBE –
DIFFERENT THEORIES CONSIDERED — EVOLUTION
OF SPECIES—LOW FORMS OF LIFE.

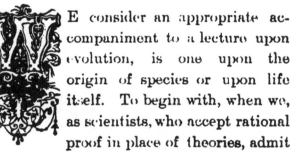 E consider an appropriate ac-
companiment to a lecture upon
evolution, is one upon the
origin of species or upon life
itself. To begin with, when we,
as scientists, who accept rational
proof in place of theories, admit
the philosophical and natural formation of
our planet from pre-existing gaseous elements, we must admit that there was a time
when there was not upon the entire globe any
living thing, even with the low form of life
possessed by the vegetable world.

The question then arises: Whence did life come? Some scientists have argued that it came from some outside source, and that the seeds of some low forms of life were brought to this planet by some meteoric rock arriving from another planet. This view is wholly inadmissible, in my opinion, from the fact that:

1. When any meteoric stone or metalic formation is moving through space at an immense velocity, as they do, it is plain that such meteor has either condensed to its present form from unappropriated matter existing within interplanetary, or interstellar spaces, or else it has formed part of the body of some planet, sun, comet or satellite, previous to the beginning of its existence as a meteor.

If the former, it could not have any organic life upon it, as a matter of course. If the latter, we must consider the force necessary to project such a body from the surface or interior of a large body to such a distance as to hurl it beyond the power of gravitation to bring it back.

We can conceive of no force capable of doing this but that of intense heat, or volcanic agency. Thus, the sun is known to hurl masses with tremendous velocity into space to distances of many hundred thousands of miles. No doubt the earth, when a white, hot body, a miniature sun to our moon, was once able to do the same. But in all these cases the fact seems plain, that such an origin precludes the supposition that such a meteor could contain organized life.

2. Granting that such life could exist and survive the tremendous cold of interplanetary space, many a hundred degrees below zero, we are then confronted with the fact that, when a meteoric body comes in contact with our atmosphere, it is instantly raised to a white heat by the tremendous vibratory forces set in action through the resistance and electric tension engendered.

This usually causes such bodies to burst into small fragments, or if the body is small, to become entirely dissipated in dust or vapor. It is manifest that all this is incompatible with the existence of organic life.

3. If we should be able to surmount these difficulties, we are no better off, for we are confronted with the question: How did life start on these other heavenly bodies, or any world or satellite? Taking all these facts into consideration, it seems to me we are driven to the inevitable conclusion that life as it exists upon this planet had its origin here. Further, each and every body in the universe that has life existing thereon in vizable organic forms, has originated said life upon its surface. Now we are in a condition to enquire as to the how and when.

Ignorant and unscientific investigators, in all ages of the world, have shirked the responsibility of this question, as they have other questions regarding the universe of matter, by dismissing it with the sweeping assertion, "God made it." God made the sun, the moon, and the stars also, is added as an important after thought. The child is taught to answer the question, " Who made you?" by " God made me," when the teacher or parent knows, as well as he knows his own name, that the child has come into the world under a natural law of being, from known conditions, pre-existent in the parents, and that the fiction of an Almighty God having anything to do with the work, except in a far-fetched and figurative sense, is like the story of Santa Claus coming down the chimney to fill the stockings of the little innocents on Christmas Eve.

God does not work without natural means and under the natural laws existing. I will defy any person on earth to show a single authentic instance of the interference of any supernatural being with the natural growth or formation of things.

As God does not make worlds or animals from nothing, or from matter that did not previously exist in a natural condition to produce such worlds or animals, nowadays, we have a perfect right as reasonable, intelligent beings, to infer that He *never* did. The Infinite is not one thing to-day, another to-morrow, remember.

Therefore, we conclude that organic life started upon the earth in just as natural a manner as rocks formed or as two chemical elements first united when conditions became favorable. As the earth cooled and the crust became thicker and thicker, different elementary bodies of simple composition formed under the law of combination. The first, were those which require a high temperature for their union.

Next came others in regular order, until oxygen and hydrogen could finally unite, not for the first time in the universe, or our solar system, but the first time upon this earth, and water was the result of the union. So organized matter began to come gradually and slowly into existence and the time arrived, after many millions of years, that a number of elements, say three, oxygen, hydrogen and carbon, united in some low form of vegetable growth, as much below our present lowest form of air-breathing plants, perhaps, as a toad-stool is lower in development than a Bartlett pear-tree.

After all these hundreds of thousands of years have passed and we are certain that millions of the lower forms of vegetable life have become extinct, we yet find forms, of undoubted vegetable growth, so low in the scale of existence, that it has been a question disputed often by naturalists in the past, as to whether such forms belonged to the mineral kingdom or not.

For many millions of years the vegetable kingdom held full sway. It had nothing else to do but improve, evolute and differentiate, under the conditions of warmth, moisture and the rich, black, carbonized soil of that period. Then it was, that the immense stores of fuel were laid down in the rocky recesses of the earth in the form of hard coal, one of the forms in which carbon appears, and the most abundant one. The air of that time would not support animal life, it was so charged with that deadly poison known as carbonic anhydride, a gas formed by the union of carbon one part with oxygen two parts.

But this deadly compound was food for plant life, and it throve and luxuriated in the dark, reeking forests without let or hinderance.

In the course of time, vegetable growth had

absorbed so much carbon from the atmosphere and deposited it together with, and
incorporated in, the bodies of untold-billions
of giant trees that became covered by sedimentary deposits, which afterwards became
slate and other stones, that the air became
capable of sustaining animal life. Not such
life as we now see, but a low form of carbonic gas-breathing animals called by the
Naturalists " Surians," cold-blooded animals
that require a limited amount of oxygen to
support life.   Fishes require but little
oxygen, and they receive that little from
water.   At one age of the earth the fish
species ruled supreme. We have an age
called the " Old Red Sandstone period,"
where the entire rock, many thousands of
feet in thickness, is full of their fossilized
remains.

At another time the age of reptiles supervened and their slimy forms ranged through
the rank, swampy forests of the period with
naught to molest them. But a fish or a
reptile could not be born from a tree or a
bush, so we know that a long age of progres-

sion was necessary before so high a development was reached. Accordingly we search
for lower forms, and we find them in prod-
igal abundance, laid down in the rocky
leaves of the earth in the form of innumerable species and varieties of coral, sponges
and other low organisms. We even find the
"connecting link" between vegetable and
animal life in a species of rooted Zoophytes
so low in the scale of animal life that they
possess roots, trunks, limbs and even flowers
so near like veritable vegetable growths as
to have at first deceived our most experienced
naturalists.

Their very name Zoo, an animal, and
Phyte, a plant, indicating their two-fold
nature. Now, friends, is it not easy to understand how all this development took place
under natural conditions? Is it not far more
reasonable than the doctrine of special creation? Is it not supported by facts? Do we
not see the same improvement and evolution
going on around us to-day? Have we not
seen the peach developed with all its luscious
sweetness, from the wild, wood-covered nec-

tarine of a thousand years ago? Have we not seen hundreds of different kinds of fowls, each kind having distinct characteristics, developed within fifty years from one species? But what is the use of multiplying examples which abound everywhere.

Explain all this as you will, and some person who scorns to read and study such masterly productions such as Darwin, Huxley and Humboldt have produced, will cry out—" Bosh! Show me where a piece of protoplasm has turned to a man, or some instance where a frog has turned into a sheep or cow, and I will believe you." What vain twaddle. Did such arguers understand but the first principles of evolution, they would know that the connecting link between a sheep and a frog, or the place where each branched from some common stock, was so far back in the geological history of this globe that the historical period of man is simply as nothing in comparison. A moment, a drop in the ocean of time. A chip from the Infinite work shop.

I have not alluded, in this lecture to the

soul or psychic force that has from the very first accompanied all this progression, and steadily progressed and gained new powers as its environments improved.   That belongs to the higher domain of metaphysical research, and I have set forth my views upon that heretofore, in the lectures entitled, "The Astral Body" and "The Soul of Man."

Of course, I cannot give anything like an exhaustive argument on such a weighty subject as this, in the short space of a single lecture.   But I trust that I have said enough to set people to thinking and to cause them to study further and thus gain a complete knowledge of this wonderful key to the universe of matter and spirit—*Infinite Evolution.*

LECTURE XII.

𝔍𝔫𝔣𝔦𝔫𝔦𝔱𝔶.

A GOD OF MERCY A CHRISTIAN CONCEPTION

The Magi and the Coming Light.

WHAT IS INFINITY?—A HARD QUESTION TO ANSWER
—FINITE MINDS CANNOT COMPREHEND THE IN-
FINITE INTELLIGENCE—ATTEMPTS TO CONCEIVE
THE INFINITE HAVE RESULTED IN CRUDE CON-
CEPTIONS OF DEITY—THE WORK WE HAVE BE-
FORE US.

THE question has often been asked of me, what do you understand by the term Infinity, so often used by you in your lectures? I will endeavor this evening to give an answer to that question, as well as I am able. At first sight it seems an easy question to answer; but on second thought, it is not so easy as it seems. Man with his finite understanding cannot comprehend Infinity, even when the term is only applied to physical elements; therefore, how much greater the difficulty becomes when he undertakes the comprehension of the Infinite Intelligence.

In all ages of the world and in all lands, whether civilized or uncivilized, men have attempted to reach outward and upward to that great and grand embodiment of power called by some the "*Soul of the Universe* ;" by others God, the great I am, and hundreds of other names that I need not particularize.

How they have most lamentably failed, can be seen, when we take a glance at the various conceptions of God, as set forth in the so-called "holy books" of various nations and religions. It is obvious that, as Col. Ingersoll justly observes, each nation makes its own God, to suit its own ideas.

Some nations evidently lacked imaginative power to such an extent that they were forced to borrow their conceptions of Deity mostly from surrounding peoples; hence we see, as in the case of the Jewish conception of Infinite Power, a being of mixed qualities, of so conglomerate a nature, that we are forced to conclude that part of the character was borrowed from the earlier astronomical religions, part from Grecian mythology and part conceived from the Jewish idea of what a great all-powerful king and despot would be.

Thus, Jehovah becomes a " consuming fire " and a " shining light," who burns up and utterly consumes his enemies. (Astronomical and sun worship.) He is also Lord of Lords and ruling God over all other Gods, of whom he is jealous, however, for fear these other gods may attract some of the adoration belonging properly to him. Of Pagan, Romish origin in all probability. He was also " Lord of Hosts," or a great leader in battle and carnage. Clearly a Grecian conception. He also becomes a being of loving and infinite mercy, who would not unjustly punish any one. This idea evidently had its rise among the early Christians, who, smarting under the laws of persecution and injustice, very natur-

ally concluded that their God was the very
opposite of the tyrannical and oppressive
Roman Emperors under whom they suffered.

The Red Man's conception of the Infinite is
a "Great Spirit" residing in the beautiful
hunting grounds of the hereafter. The wild
Indian had no idea of kings, tyrants, thrones
and kneeling courtiers. *His* life was spent
in the grand isles of the forest, amid sparkling lakes and on the banks of babbling
brooks and rushing rivers; therefore his
conceptions of the Deity differed in many
respects from that of the more civilized
nations. In fact, many scientific men agree
in thinking that the Aborigines, through
their nearness to "Nature's heart," so to
speak, have arrived at a more rational theory
of Divinity than have their pale faced
brothers.

Where man has failed in his conception of
the Infinite, is in attributing such finite
qualities to such a power.

Think of learned men, in all seriousness,
teaching such utter nonsense as, that God
made the world out of nothing, or spake it

into existence, or that he went at it and made a man out of dust and a woman from a rib of the same man! What childish thoughts these are, worthy of the barbarians who originated them.

You see, these ignorant men could make a hatchet out of a stone, by patient labor; so, when they saw things existing which were evidently formed in an intelligent manner, they concluded that some great powerful man must have made them. They reasoned thus: Here are men; there must have been a first man to start the race. Now, who made him? "Why, God did of course." That settled it! No use to look any further. No use of a Humboldt or a Darwin studying and delving into nature's laws. No use of digging into the earth, examining the leaves of countless stratifications of rock! No use of geology or astronomy! Why should Darwin study out the "descent of man," or Proctor the formation of worlds, when the whole thing was settled once for all by Moses? Yes, God made the heavens and the earth. Yes, "And the stars also." That was highly satisfactory in old times, and has continued to be taught down to our own enlightened nineteenth century.

That kind of pap may do for weak-minded men, women and children; but thinking people have long since outgrown such absurdities.

The fact slowly dawned upon the minds of thinking men, that " nothing " was a poor quality of timber for even a God to make a world from. They realized that no person had ever seen a " creation " of anything, however small, and therefore, reasoning from analogy, they concluded that there had never been a creation, but always a constant round of transformation.

That was the key note of knowledge. The great principle of evolution once discovered, man was in a condition to investigate the laws of the Infinite. The geologist with his hammer; the astronomer with his telescope; the chemist with his retort, and scientists in all the co-ordinate branches of knowledge, could step to the front and find the underlying laws that have been acting through all time to produce what is.

They could be no longer stopped by the childish answer—" God made it." But I have not answered the question—

WHAT IS INFINITY?

It is far easier to tell what it is *not*, than what it *is*.   It cannot be a man or a woman or any being like unto a mixture of the two with " parts and passions." Why? Because the moment we set up such a being anywhere in space, say within our solar system, for instance, we are confronted with the absurdity that he, she or it, is at an infinite distance from all other points in thousands and millions of directions.

Why should such a being choose this particular system as a residence from among the millions and billions of brilliant orbs that hold sway over countless inhabitable globes in this and other clusters of suns?

Why should an Infinite and all-powerful man, or a God of the same pattern, concern himself so very particularly over the affairs of this particular little mustard seed of a globe, that is, after all, nothing but a grain of sand on the shores of eternity? If he ever made the earth, he must have made all. If he ever constructed a *first* one—where did he stay, and what did he do during countless billions of ages that constituted a small fraction of the eternity of time that preceded that first globe-making?

"Oh, but," said my clerical friend the other day, "Perhaps God did not live during all that long time." All right, then, but who made him? That is the question. If he ever had a starting-point, some intelligent being must have created him, according to your theory—if all organized things must have a creator. No, my friend, there is no half-way to this business. We cannot comprehend the Infinite, but we can use our reason in such a manner as to reach out part way upon the road toward the Infinite. We can reason that space is Infinite, from our inability to conceive of an end to it. From the very nature of *time*, it could have no beginning or end. In the same way we reason that matter, and therefore worlds and

suns, always existed, because we cannot conceive of a time when the same causes that
now operate to produce worlds were not
operating and producing. We further
reason that the Infinite Intelligence, or the
Spirit of the Universe, always existed, from
our total inability of conceiving the starting
or creation of such a being.

So it is almost wholly as a species of negative reasoning that we arrive at our theories
of the Infinite. Mathematics reach out *toward*
infinity, but do not, and cannot arrive at the
end, for there is no end to arrive at. We can
indicate infinity in certain directions. Take
the unit one, the emblem of the universe. Divide this by two, and we have the fraction one
half. Keep on dividing the quotient arising,
and we get the series one-half, one-fourth, one-
eighth, one-sixteenth, etc., to infinity, as the
denominator gets larger and larger. Multiply
the unit by two, and keep on multiplying the
product arising therefrom by two, and we get
the series two, four, eight, sixteen, etc., up to
infinity. We now have infinity in two directions from unity *in one plane only*. Depart

from this plane, and our figures become finite.
For instance. take our last term, sixteen, and
begin to subtract from it any modicum, how-
small, and you arrive ultimately at an extinc-
tion of the number. Therefore this kind of
infinity is not the kind that we spell with a
capital I.

No number, however large, can reach out to
infinity. Set up a row of figures that standing
side by side, would reach from the earth to the
orbit of Neptune, and then conceive of a being
who would be capable in the fullness of time,
of making a journey directly off in space, that
number of miles. Think you he would then
be "Beyond the bounds of time and space?"
No! he would still be as far from the end as
ever, for still out and ahead would extend the
vast universe of space, still studded with clusters
of suns and nebula.

Still would he find the reign of law and
crder; still would vibrate and palpitate the
wonderful forces that constitute the manifestation of the Infinite. Therefore I conclude that
Infinity consists of a universal intelligence
that has no up or down, no in our out, no be-

ginning or end, no parts or passions, but extends in all directions to an infinite distance, and comprises all there is and all there ever will be.

"But, see here," says my materialistic friend, "that is just about my definition of nothing, or empty space; so what authority have you for calling this thing a Universal Intelligence?"

I can only answer this question in one way: We know that man and other animals have an attribute that we call intelligence, that enables them to adapt certain means to certain ends. We look around us and we see that over and above this finite intelligence of ours, there is an intelligence that adapts certain means to certain ends, independent of man's intelligence. Reasoning from this fact, we deduce the theory that there is a higher intelligence, of which man has always been dimly cognizant, but has greatly erred in giving this manifestly Infinite Intelligence crude finite attributes.

This God needs no army of priests to interpret his will. He does not become angry or jealous. He never had to send his only begotten son to die on the cross to appease his own wrath. He never ordered innocent maidens sacrificed to the lust of a rabble horde of men, called soldiers. He never cared how Moses cut his clothes; or how Aaron cut his beard, or whether Lot's poor wife was "looking backward" or not. I firmly believe that men have invented these tales out of their own crude, finite understanding and have palmed them off upon the ignorant and credulous masses as gospel truth.

Thousands and tens of thousands of priests and preachers have lived on the fat of the land while teaching these absurd doctrines to their dupes. They will continue to do so for a long time to come. But here and there has arisen thinkers who cannot be kept in the old leading strings. They see the error and darkness of the past. They seek the light of knowledge and understanding. and look upward toward the sparkling dawn. They realize that the universe has a *soul*, and that they, too, have a soul. Yes, a soul to save. To save from what? From darkness, from the outer darkness of ignorance.

It is in vain that the "old serpent" says of the Tree of Knowledge: "In the day that thou eatest therefore thou shalt surely die." They can not be frightened by that bugaboo any longer. They have outgrown it. They are no longer children, but full grown, thinking men and women.

It is a part of the work of the Ancient Order of the Magi, which I have the honor of representing in this age, to teach mankind the true conception of the Infinite. To help them raise their minds and hearts upward out of the slough of ignorance and error of the dark ages, and to give them a true understanding of the laws that govern men and things. Our aim is to give men a true conception of infinite love, harmony and life, and to restore a portion of that lost "Light of Egypt" formerly reflected from Atlantis. We do not antagonize other organizations, that have their own work, their own way, of helping in the general uplifting of humanity.

The symbolism of the Masonic Fraternity, when properly understood, wlll be found to be in exact harmony with our teachings.

Their symbols are astronomical, their conceptions of the Infinite Ruler are the same as ours, when taken in their pure sense.

We should all work together.

In doing this, our allotted work, we hope and trust that we are raising men higher and higher, nearer and nearer toward the "Great White Throne," eternal on high, the seat of everlasting judgment, the Soul of the Universe, the ever-existing, omnipresent, over-ruling Intelligence that we call INFINITY.

LECTURE XIII.

Study of Infinity.

HOW MEN HAVE ATTEMPTED TO GAIN KNOWLEDGE OF THE INFINITE.

Fallacy of Special Revelation.

ALL SORTS OF GODS—GROTESQUE IDEAS OF THE DEITY—GODS MADE TO ORDER—TRUTH HAS A CONSTANT WARFARE—HELL FIRE COOLING OFF—THE TRUE BOOK OF THE INFINITE PAGES OF LIVING LIGHT—THE GRAND DIVINE REVELATION—THE RIGHT BOOK TO STUDY—THE ROCK OF WISDOM.

UPWARD through the ages from time immemorial men have sought to know of the mysterious being who has been called by the name of God, Allah, Ra, Ammon, Osiris, Tao, Juggernaut, Odin, Helios and a host of other names that I cannot recall. There is a law that seems well-nigh universal, that when a demand exists in the minds of men for anything, some one or something will arrive to fill the want. The article furnished to satisfy the demand is generally the best that can be furnished at the stage of development to which the world or the nation has arrived at the time. To draw a material analogy, take window-panes. Light was needed in dwellings in former times as much as it is now; but the best articles that were available were the semi-opaque skins of certain animals or the thin membraneous portion of certain internal organs of those animals. Oiled paper was used and oiled silk, with more or less success, up to the time when glass came into use and furnished just the article needed. One having close texture, hard surface and other good qualities, combined with the useful property of being nearly transparent. The man would be thought crazy now who would fit up his windows with the best article procurable by kings and emperors a few hundred years ago.

It has been exactly the same with the demand for knowledge of the Creator. It must be satisfied, and, therefore, certain persons in all ages and in all countries have come to the front and invented and furnished the best knowledge procurable at the time. I say "invented," because everything goes to prove that the Gods of all nations have been invented either by accident or design, just as window-glass and its forerunners were invented. Some, and in fact nearly all, conceptions of the Deity have been a steady growth by successive additions and inventions, just as the modern self-binding reaper has been developed from the humble "Cradle" or still lower "sickle" of our grandfather's days.

Whereas men have, as a rule, been ready to accept the more enlightened improvements of material things, there has always been a strange tendency of mankind to refuse the improvements upon anything that interested parties have labeled "holy" or "sacred." These trade-marks have always been a better protection to creeds and inventions of men than the word "patented" is upon a machine.

Presuming upon this peculiar phrase of

human character, the most grotesque, unreasonable, unproveable and incomprehensible
Gods have been foisted upon the credulity
of men.   Wooden gods; duck-headed gods;
three-headed gods; one-eyed gods; angry
gods; jealous gods; murderous gods; war-like
gods; peaceful gods; double gods; triple gods
and a host of others which are far too numerous to mention.

Each nation has seemed to endeavor to outdo all others, by incorporating into their
conception of the Deity all, or nearly all, the
grotesque ideas of preceding religions, and
then adding to the sum total any particular
quality that they could originate with credit
to their conception, or with a view to making
their God more acceptable to the people. A
god once set up in business, the next thing
needed was a full and accurate account of how
he made this world and the heavens and "all
the parts of them." Here was a good chance
for monks, priests, writers and what not,
to indulge their fancy to the utmost, and we
have had the most foolish, utterly false and
incredible statements promulgated as gospel

truth that ever could emanate from the
brains of men perfectly ignorant of nature
and the underlying laws of the universe.

Every scientific truth that has been discovered by the patient and unselfish delvers
into the secrets of nature, has had to fight its
way step by step against the swift current of
public opinion and belief engendered by the
ignorant teachings of former ages.   The very
men who would not think of using the tools
or inventions of their grandfathers' days, are
contented to accept the god, heaven, purga-
tery, hell and devils of two thousand years
ago.

It is very true. though, that the preachers
and teachers of this rubbish do their utmost
to improve upon these crude notions and conceptions of former ages, but they are so bound
down by their creeds, holy books and opinions
of those formerly in authority, that the work
goes on but slowly.   Still they are evoluting
more rapidly now than at any other period of
the world's history.   Within my recollection
the church doctrines have changed wonderfully.   I have heard ministers of the gospel

stand up in the pulpit and preach the most lurid hell-fire-and-brimstone sermons imaginable, winding up with a glowing picture of your friends and relations who had "sinned away the day of grace," roasting in that immeasureable gulf of fire, in view of the "redeemed ones" looking over the battlements of heaven. The preacher who would dare preach such doctrines now would either find his church deserted, or he would get a polite hint that he was too much of a way-back to suit the tastes of that congregation.   But it is all in their creeds yet.

They ignore it, but it is there.

The same old stories of the creation are in the bible, but they smooth them over and try to explain them away.

Now, my friends, as I have at some length exhibited the fallacies of the past regarding this great subject, it is only right that I should tell you where to look and what book to study in order to gain correct knowledge of the infinite God whom most men concede the existence of.

I consider it usless to advise you to place

confidence in any so-called "Divine revelation," said to have been given to any man or set of men in past times, for the reason that each and every revelation purporting to have come direct from the Almighty hand, from our earlest records up to that of Brigham Young, have contained such gross errors regarding well known scientific facts, as to forever place them outside the pale of belief of thinking and intelligent persons.

The question now arises: How has God revealed himself to us, and how can we find Him and know of Him?

Friends, He has written a book, a grand and beautiful book. It is bound in the blue of ethereal space, and is illuminated with hundreds of millions of sparkling suns that trace in letters of living light the story of creation. Some chapters of this wondrous book are made up of thousands of rocky leaves, where we may read the history of how this old earth was made and the history of nations of denizens that have succeeded each other on its surface. The illustrations in this geological chapter are the most trustworthy pictures we could possess, being the actual bodies of these ancient beings preserved and incased in living rock.

Some chapters must be read with the aid of the microscope, others with the telescope and spectroscope; but read as we may and study as we may, we find an endless and infinite fund of knowledge, fresh to our hands, shining on every page with glittering lines of fact and truth. We need never fear that we will exhaust this book; it is infinite.

We may not always translate the mystic pages of this wonderful book correctly, from lack of knowledge and understanding of its language and hidden meaning.

But the book is not in fault. On re-reading it, we see beauty, order and harmony where we failed to see them before, and we can correct our former errors. Therefore, I charge you, brethren, as true and worthy mystics, to study well this great and grand book of real Divine Revelation. Pry into its hidden mysteries, its inmost secrets.

Penetrate behind the veil that hides the temple of the Unknown from the eyes of the profane. Possess yourself of the golden key that unlocks the Mystic Temple of Light.

Perservere in this; you will never regret it, and you will have the supreme satisfaction of knowing that you have not founded your faith upon the treacherous quicksands of man-made theories, but have builded it upon the solid rock of Divine and Infinite Wisdom.

LECTURE XIV.

The Order of the Magi.

WHY IT HAS EXPERIENCED A REVIVAL IN THIS CENTURY.

THE BROTHERHOOD OF MAGIC—THE TRUTH ALWAYS DISTASTEFUL TO A LARGE PART OF MANKIND—THE "THREE WISE MEN"—FOLLOWING A STAR—THE TRUTH SUPPRESSED BY THE PRIESTHOOD—THE MAGI, THE CONSERVATORS OF TRUE HISTORY—THE GREAT MASONIC DEPARTURE—KEEPERS OF THE WORD—LANDMARK OF PROPHECY—THE COMING LIGHT.

E have had hundreds of questions asked covering these points, and we will answer them as plainly as possible. The order has always, since its very inception, ages and ages ago, dealt in magic, in mystic emblems and

numbers.   The name Magi, plural, and
magus, singular, and Magea, a commander
in magic, all come from the same root.   All
that was wonderful in nature, and at the
same time not generally understood, was regarded as mystical, and therefore, magical,
and came within the province of this order.

For thousands and thousands of years the
priests and masters of mystic lore were a
power in the land.   They were the conservators of knowledge that had been gathered by
patient and laborious research, carried on by
sworn brothers, through a period of time
which compared with our so-called historical
epoch, was long.   Knowing the magic power
possessed by these masters, even kings feared
them, and therefore sought to placate them
by grants of money, lands and emoluments.

From the books handed down to us from
past times, we can gain but little true history
of this wonderful order, for the very good
reason that the manuscripts, scrolls, etc.,
which did give a true history, have been
hidden and destroyed; while the ones preserved were invariably written by enemies of

the order, to-wit, the church. By "the church" we do not mean any particular religious body, but all dealers in so-called "revealed" religion.

Inasmuch as the fundamental belief and teaching of the Magi has always been that the "universe is governed by law," a doctrine that has been enunciated by thousands of philosophers in our own day, it has, of course, followed that the dealers in a system that teaches that the universe is governed by capricious gods and devils, that can be placated or subsidized, by properly approaching them, into changing the natural course of nature, have invariably been our bitter enemies.

What else could be expected? The truth has always been bitter to a large proportion of mankind. Let any man promulgate a new system of philosophy, and he was rewarded with a cup of poison, the stake, or the dungeon. Every newly-found truth must run the gauntlet of scorn and villification. It is even so unto this day, only the teeth and claws of the monster, Ignorance, have been

blunted to such an extent that they cannot
rend and tear as in days of yore.

After the fall of Atlantis, Egypt became
the theatre of the exploits of the Brotherhood of Magic, and they arose, during a
period of several thousands of years, to a
position nearly as grand as that once reached
by their brothers of Atlantis. Everything
that could be written or said to belittle this
noble order, was industriously gathered and
saved; but in spite of all, a little here and a
little there, of fact, has crept into ancient
writings, prophecies, etc., which show to us a
glimpse of the truth.

Do you suppose for a moment that the
church would have allowed the account to
pass into history, of the fact that Jesus was
discovered by a committee of three of the so-
called "wise men of the East," had it not
have been in their anxiety to obtain proofs of
the divinity of Jesus, of which they were
sorely in need? And see how the account
has been garbled by the rendering. Instead
of stating the fact, which was that the Magi
followed the teachings of the stars in the

finding of Jesus, and took their direction of travel from a certain star while making that long and eventful journey, we have the absurd statement that they "followed a star," which evidently, according to the text, went ahead, and "stood over" the child until the brothers caught up (Math. 9, 10.)

Then again, how much pains have been taken to conceal the fact that Jesus was taken to Egypt and there became learned in the science and knowledge of past ages, to be found only within the sacred temples of the magi. That would never do, to admit that Jesus received his knowledge, and, therefore, power, from the magi, would be fatal to the pretensions of the parties interested.

Consequently, every one of the " gospels " extant up to the year A. D. 400, that set forth the facts in the case, were suppressed. Some of these gospels relate, in a minute manner the childhood of Jesus and his life in Egypt. But, strange to say, the gospel, according to Mathew was allowed to remain, where a short account is given of the arrival of the wise men and the departure of Jesus for Egypt (Math.

II, 10 to 15.)   St. Luke says (I, 80): "And the child grew, and waxed strong in spirit, and was *in the deserts* till the day of his shewing unto Israel."   In other words, Jesus was away beyond certain desert countries in Egypt until he was a full-grown man.

Mark and John quietly skip over all responsibility by bringing Jesus onto the stage of action and full manhood.   It is wonderful, though, how a reading between the lines will reveal to a Mystic so much that the church could not understand.   Read St. John I, 14, and see how that writer regarded Christ as a fleshy reprosentative of the *Word*; in other words, a possessor of the sacred word.

In later years, scientific writers of textbooks for our schools, in their anxiety to cater to the believers in supernatural religion, have deliberately suppressed facts regarding the deep knowledge possessed by our sacred order in ancient times.   In not one astronomy of a later date than 1840, that I have ever seen, can be found an acknowledgement that the true system of the motion of the planets about the sun was known and taught in the temples of Egypt ages before the days of Copernicus, whom they credit with the discovery; but in astronomical works published prior to 1840, credit is given where it belongs. Ryan's astronomy, a very exhaustive work on mathematical astronomy, published, I think in 1831, is one of the works that honestly gives due credit to the Magi. For more minute reference to this, see lecture "Looking Backward."

It has always been easy for the promulgators of falsehood to suppress the advocates of truth. By a strange law of nature, the truth always has to stand on its own merits. Those who stand for the truth never "strike back." Did you ever hear of a person being tortured on the rack to make him admit a belief in a scientific truth? Was a man ever burned at the stake because he would not believe that the earth was round, or that the sun was the true center of our system? Never! While the supporters of lies have carried them to the hearts of the people upon the points of millions of blood-dripping swords, spears and bayonets, the advocates of truth have quietly plodded onward, secretly meeting in caves and

underground crypts, ever satisfied that in time
truth would prevail.   And they were right.   It
will prevail in the long run.

As regards scientific facts, we might say
relative to the average churchman:

> Truth presents to us so frightful a mien,
> That to be hated needs but to be seen;
> But seen too oft, encountered face to face,
> We hesitate, then pity, then embrace.

Every scientific truth has had to run the
gauntlet of: "That does not agree with our
holy scriptures."   But we notice that when
the fact is so firmly established that there is
no shaking it; our theologians quickly discover
that it " agrees exactly with scripture."

Had not the true and original *secret order*,
based upon astral law, been changed into an
order that professed to take its inspiration from
the Jewish bible, and did substitute words
taken from that book for the true, grand word
and all the minor pass-words, we would not
have to-day the great and grand order denominated Masonry; which order has preserved
much to us that would otherwise have been
lost.   The Egyptian branch, that did preserve

the ancient landmarks and keep to the sacred teachings of our order, were scattered to the four winds of heaven, and reduced to a few here and a few there, who were sworn to, and did, transmit the secret doctrines from mouth to ear down through all the dark centuries of ignorance that supervened.

Even the Masonic departure, which took place at the building of King Solomon's Temple, came very near being annihilated during certain periods. The church was ever suspicious of the lodge; but, by adding new degrees from time to time, that catered more and more to the church, the leaders of the order have managed to keep it up. Change it however, as they may, the old harlot of Revelation will not recognize it, and many of her children follow her lead.

As a fraternal association the Masonic order is a decided success, both morally and financially; but as an association reaching beyond mere earthly things and fitting one for the great hereafter, its most ardent devotees would hardly claim it.

As the secret knowledge of the Magi has

handed down the ages from one unto
ther, the ones who have held their place in
line have been called the "Keepers of the
rd." In some instances the number of
epers" have fallen so low as three, although
ffort has been made to keep the number up
even at all times.

ars and pestilence have sometimes nearly
off the succession, but according to ancient
hecy the secret doctrines have been kept
down to this day, when the "books
to be opened" and "certain signs' should
cate the coming of light once more to
earth.

hen the writer was approached by the
her in Nashville, Tenn., in 1864, he had
more knowledge of mystic light than a
d. Even after I had been instructed in
Word and its use, and initiated as well as
umstances would admit, as a mystic, all
yet blind, and I was obliged to await the
when more would be unfolded to me
t time arrived without volition on my part,
all was brought about in accordance with
phetic records.

How surprised we are, when we find that what we have been doing apparently with perfect freedom of will, was all foreordained, as it were, and predicted years before. We ought not to be surprised at it, but we cannot help it. We are all instruments for the operation of divine law, and we cannot but fulfill our destiny. The one who is called upon to fill the highest place in the glorious work deserves no more praise than he who fills the lowest place. It is his destiny, that is all.

Why has the light of Oriental Mysticism come back to the world just at this time? The answer is this: Because the world was not in a condition to receive it before. Certain mathematical knowledge had to come first; certain astronomical discoveries and certain instruments had to be made; some person must be born who had a combination of certain qualities necessary in the work; not better or grander qualities than those possessed by millions of others, but peculiar in their combination.

Then, lastly, the world must be slowly prepared for the light. This preparation has been going on steadily since 1833, when the last sign in the heavens came to pass.   The year 1844 was another landmark of ancient prophecy, and the culmination of the out-pouring of the spirit for forty-five years took place in 1889, when the books were opened and the first modern temple established upon the earth.

The "Star of the East" once more rises to guide the mystic traveler upon his way; while the light of the rising sun guilds the pyramids of Egypt with a Golden Light.

LECTURE XV.

What the Magi Teach.

THE CLASS OF PEOPLE THEY APPEAL TO.

The Universal Principal - The Great Magnet
— Folly of Creeds — The Reli .ion of Blood—
Materialism Run Mad - Spiri .ism Gone Crazy
- Transcendentalism, Christian Science, and
Theosophy Considered — Erronious Spiritual
Teachings—The Secret Doctr.ne, What is it
—Light of Atlantis and America.

HIS is a subject of vital importance to all those who take an
interest in the order and think
of becoming members. The Magi
believe and teach that the Universe is made up of two great
principles of an opposite nature, namely,
spirit and matter. We might say psychic

force and material force, although the terms are more obscure, because all matter and all spirit are simply forms of vibratory force. These two great principles are like opposite polarities of the same magnet. Both poles belong to the same magnet and meet and neutralize in the middle thereof, yet the manifestations are different and in fact quite opposite in some particulars.

Thus we find that the terms spirit and matter stand for one great universal principle with two polarities.

We teach that intelligent beings must recognize both states of the principle, and that any system of philosophy that does not recognize these facts, is defective, and must fall sooner or later. To spirit belongs the high and fine vibratory forces that constitute the mind, intelligent, thought, emotion, etc., that go to make up the spirit side of man. The material belongs to the lower vibratory forces that constitute the body we live in, and through which the indwelling spirit or soul makes itself manifest.

Just so the whole universe—for man is a

type or epitome of the universe—is made up
of these two great principles.

> " The universe is one stupendous whole,
> Whose body nature is and God the soul."

This oft-quoted couplet is a grand fact, and a
man wrote it who had the true mystic mind.
The great trouble of mankind in all ages has
been to properly separate these two principles, giving both their true signification
and not mixing them up in their systems of
philosophy and religion. The speaker has
been astounded many times by the utter
lack of all understanding of the true nature
of various causes and effects, evinced by
many persons and even entire schools. For
instance, the Christian and Jewish faiths
mix spirit and matter most wonderfully.
God, who, as the Infinite, occupies the most
ultra spirit end of the *spectrum celestia*, is
believed in as a material being with limbs,
" parts and passions," and occupying a
material throne in a material heaven, with
streets paved with one of the materials which
belong at the other end among the most
ponderable bodies, to wit, gold.

The part saved of man, when he becomes finally fit to enter this material heaven, is nothing but the body. The body—the blood—is the burden of the scriptures. Is it any wonder that a certain popular preacher said a few years ago: "If you mark all the passages of the scriptures that speak of blood with red ink, you will find the sacred book a stream of blood from end to end."

Christ, a pure principle, meaning the same as Christna of the Hindus or Osiris of the Egyptians, is made to be, and is, worshiped as a material being. If this is not genuine materialism, and a materialism run mad at that, then what is it?

On the other hand, certain actions of men which have their origin in purely material surroundings and belong on the material plane, are erroneously ascribed to "bad spirits" or devils. Fits or spasms caused by an irritation in the spine, or by worms in the intestinal canal, were called spirits, or the work of spirits, "and cast out" by charms and incantations. If this is not Spiritism; and a mad article at that, what is it?

But the church-man is not the only one who confounds this great principle in its two modes of manifestation. The ordinary material philosopher, or so-called scientist, looks only at the material universe, and denies everything that he cannot see, feel or weigh. He denies spirit or any intelligent force or vibration only that of matter. Some materialists are so set in their belief that all a person has to do is to let them know that he believes in a future state of existence to be set down as a crank, almost outside the pale of human sympathy.

As an offset to this class, we have the new schools of transcendentalism and Christian science, who go to the other extreme and declare that matter does not exist—matter is all moonshine. We think we exist on a world, but it is a huge mistake. We think a part of our so-called system is out of order and think we have a pain, but we have no system and no pain. "There is nothing material."

Of course I am giving only the views of the most *ultra* teachers of these schools. Ah! my good friends, I love you and respect you, but

I fear me you are too much to the other end of
the great magnet. Another great class that
have come to the front during the last few
years, and have been especially prolific in literature, is the Theosophist. This school of
thinkers have a vein of spiritual truth running
all the way through their teachings that in a
measure leavens the whole lump; but I trust
that all of that school who read this, will forgive me when I say that the mixing of spirit
and what is of spirit, with matter and what is
of matter, is very great in nearly all theosophic
works.

Within the past week I have read in a theosophic work by a noted writer, that "the earth
itself may be thrown out of her just equilibrium
of forces by the stupendous will perversions of
of an earthly potentate," etc. My friends,
when this old earth is thrown out of her
equilibrium of forces, such as magnetism and
gravatic forces, or, in fact, any other natural
force through the power of any man's will, I
want to be there to see it.

In the same book, which I open at random,
I find that "The Atlantians, gradually becom-

ing addicted to the practice of an infernal
magic, used their super-physical powers un-
lawfully. They allied themselves with death
instead of with life, co-operating with nature
on her side of destruction; and thus, we are
told, brought upon themselves the engulfing
floods of oblivion.

What a far-fetched spiritual reason to give
a catastrophe that was as natural and material
in its nature as is the fall of an over-ripe apple
or a dead leaf. Atlantis sank beneath the
waves of the Atlantic Ocean, as Mr. Donnelly
so ably shows, under the same material forces,
aquaus and volcanic, that have heretofore and
will hereafter level continents, raise islands and
otherwise change the face of the world.

What is the use of attributing a spiritual
origin to a natural material state of matter?
Matter and spirit have always existed in perfect correlation to each other. One has just
as much right to exist as the other. and we
must recognize the fact.

I have also found the most astounding
theories abounding in Theosophic works relative to the nature of man's spirit. "Shells"

and "astral envelopes," over-souls and in-souls, and several other parts of man's spirit, floating about on earth and in the heavens. My dear friends, I do not say one word against those who believe and teach such doctrines; I do not set down one word in malice, but for heaven's sake do not trouble your heads over any such complicated spirit to man. Ask those who teach it to prove it.

Another thing I must call your attention to is the erroneous teachings of some Spiritualists. I allude to no particular one. Some teach that the only thing really worth knowing is spirit. Let a scientist endeavor, after years of study of the subject, to show that the fact of man's future existence is perfectly consonant and harmonious with true science, and that the more we know of the scientific laws that govern matter and mind, the more we know regarding a future state of life; let him, as I say, endeavor to instill this truth into the minds of men and many will cry out in public and private: "Oh he is on the material plane," or "science is the greatest enemy of Spiritualism."

Friends, I don't deny it. Science is the

greatest foe the churches ever had; but Spiritualism need not fear science. Science is nothing but demonstrated truth, and truth can hurt no true and good thing. The only thing a truth will not fit into is an untruth. Truth fits truth like the stones in the Pyramid of Cheops, square and true, jointed like a fine piece of cabinet work.

A three-cornered lie may be made to fit in for a time, by plastering it well with the plaster of sophistry and the cement of ignorance, but as soon as investigation is made with the hammer of science the cement loosens and the stone falls from its place, leaving a hole in the structure.

The people we appeal to for our work are those who have advanced to a point where the ism they have hitherto professed does not seem to fill their hearts and souls. We do not ask any person to give up a single good or a single truth. Keep all you have and add all the good and true you can get thereunto.

THE SECRET DOCTRINE; WHAT IS IT?

It is Christianity, with the absurdities of a bodily resurrection, a material heaven, an

endless hell and many others matters of the
kind left out. It is Theosophy, with the wild
and untenable speculations of dreamers and
absurdities wrapped in uncouth Sanscrit and
Hindoo terms. to conceal their nakedness,
omitted. It is Spiritualism of the highest
type, with the false communication and ignorant teachings of unadvanced beings on the
other side ignored. It is science, minus the
short-sighted and unscientific mode of invest-
gation, which places a limit on infinity and
stops short at the point where man's very
limited physical senses cease.

It is Transcendentalism in its best form,
which ignores nothing real, while giving due
prominence to will force and mind, or the
psychic powers. It also takes due cognizance
of the physical universe, without which spirit
could not manifest itself or gain in progressive knowledge or experience.

In short, we appeal to that large and growing class of thinkers who have become tired
of old theories and have therefore arrived at
a fit state of development to appreciate the
Light of Atlantis and America.

LECTURE XVI.

Needs of Mankind.

Man Needs Advancement in Light, or Knowledge of the Infinite Laws and Powers that Govern the Earth and Its Inhabitants.

IGNORANCE OF PRETENDERS TO DIVINE KNOWLEDGE - TRIAL BY FAITH PROVES NOTHING - THE ORDER OF THE MAGI NEVER PERSECUTES FOR OPINION'S SAKE - HOW THE TRUTH CUTS THE LATER COURTS OF EGYPT—THE ORDER HAS COME AGAIN TO STAY.

RIGHTLY speaking, the only progress ever made by man has come through increase of human knowledge of this kind. But, first, let us define what this knowledge consists of. It is conceded by all, or nearly all intelligent thinkers, that God himself is beyond our

reach. We who believe that God is Infinite,
can believe no other way, inasmuch as it is
utterly impossible for a finite being to comprehend, understand or cognize an infinite
being or organization.

This being the case, then how can we gain
knowledge and light of and concerning God?
By just one way, and that is by studying
the phenomena of the universe and the laws
of life and existence.

When an astronomer examines and studies
a far-off star, and learns its dimensions, distance and physical constitution, he does not
see the sun or star itself, but simply the light
that is caused by vibrations set up, in some
cases many years before, by the tremendous
forces at work upon that sun.

No telescope ever yet made by man can
raise the disk of a star so that it can be seen
as a globe. Magnify it as we may, we still
see but the pencil of light that alone bears
its message to us, pulsating through space
with the well-nigh incomprehensible velocity
of over one hundred and eighty thousand
miles per second.

Thus it is with our knowledge of God. To study God we must study his works. To study his works we must study science. Scientific knowledge is simply classified, proven, and the best knowledge obtainable in regard to natural phenomena.

Would you know how the earth was made, read the leaves of the great geological book of the earth's stratified rocks.

Would you know how man was made, read the record as inscribed upon those pages in fossilized remains of animals long ago extinct.

Would you know how the universe was made, read it in the starry heavens where countless billions of suns speak to you in letters of fire.

Would you know the nature of life and motion, of death and decay, of the now and the hereafter, of the very soul forces in man and what governs and controls such forces, study the all-prevading vibratory motions that are about us and within us, and you have the key that unlocks the mysteries of the Infinite..

What gave the world the enormous benefits

of steam, power electric communication, electro-motor force, and a thousand other things that contribute daily and hourly to our comfort and high state of civilization? Simply a true knowledge of some of the attributes of the Almighty; a knowledge of some of the vibratory forces of the universe. Therefore we claim that we are students of the only kind of knowledge that leads man up towards the Infinite God. We believe that those who claim to have direct dealings with God, or to act as vicegerents on earth to represent God, are false teachers. They know no more about God than does the ignorant Fejee Islander, who worships a stone or a tree under the belief that it is a supernatural being.

The difference is one of degree only. The general tendency of man, as he rises in knowledge of nature's governing forces, is to put God at a greater and greater distance. Races that have developed but little above the beasts have a stone god in their very hut or cave of habitation. Higher in the scale we find nations believing in many gods, but placing them above the clouds. Later they got down to one

God and he was in some place called a heaven, far above the clouds. Now, the believers in a personal god hardly know what to believe. They hate to confine their God to this one earth, or this one solar system, among the billions and trillions of systems of suns and worlds that are known to exist; but on the other hand they dislike to make him everywhere alike, or omnipresent, because in doing this they are advancing to a plane of thought far above the plane where the church stands, and are, in fact, admitting the liberal view or scientific view of God; and to this they must come in time.

Many ministers of the church have come to such an understanding of the true nature of the Infinite that they are no longer fit to remain in the iron-bound pulpits of the church to dispense musty and exploded theories of ignorant theologians of the dark ages; so they are being thrown out one by one to swell the ranks of the thinkers and truthseekers.

Therefore we claim that the need of humanity in this enlightened nineteenth century is more science and less guesswork; more truth and less theology of the dogmatic kind; more

real knowledge of the universe and less of
mythical heavens and hells; more knowledge
of an Infinite omnipresent God and less of local and man-made gods, and more trial by
proof and less trial by faith. Trial by faith
proves nothing. A hundred million people
believed the earth to be the center of the universe, and had unbounded faith in, that the
cosmogony of Moses was the truth, while one
man, Copernicus, maintained the contrary,
and placed the earth in its true relation as a
simple satellite of the sun.

The church cried "heresy!" and the gaping
jaws of the dungeons of the Inquisition opened
to receive the bold scientist, but it turned out
that the one man was right and the faith of
the hundred thousand wrong, and this the
church had to acknowledge at last. So faith
proves nothing.

This fact has always been one of the recognized tenets of the Magi. Not a member of
the order, from the highest to the lowest, is
ever required to believe anything that he does
not consider proven by facts. We have no
"believe or be damned" in our our organization.

So it is useless for inquirers to ask such questions as "What am I required to believe if I join your order?" or "Will I be obliged to give up my other societies or work?" as we require nothing of the kind.

The Order of the Magi never yet persecuted any one for opinion's sake. Those who become angry because their particular doctrines are not received by others, show at once that they themselves are suspicious that they cannot prove what they claim.

This state of things has always been a characteristic of theology. If you wish to test the truth of this, try it upon some minister or ardent church member.

Say to him: "The church has no power nowadays. You claim that you have thousands of churches and a great membership, but you have not; you are nowhere." Say this and he will laugh at you. Why? because he knows that you are wrong, and he cares no more about it than do we when some ignorant person says that the earth is flat or square, or the sun no bigger than a wagon-wheel.

But say to the same person: "The Bible

is simply a man-made book, and full of errors, and there is no proof whatever that Jesus Christ is the Son of God, or that God is three in one." Say this, and see him jump and grow red in the face, and probably refuse to talk to you. And if you happen to be the proprietor of a corner grocery you will soon notice that the members of his church do not trade with you. Now, why is this? Simply because he knows in his inmost heart that *you are right*, and he does not want to hear the truth.

This reminds me of the old fellow who was running for office in a Western state some years ago. The opposition paper came out with a story to the effect that the candidate murdered a former wife while he was a resident of Ohio a few years before. The old fellow, who had never had but one wife, and she was yet alive and well, made merry over this campaign-lie and showed it to all his friends in great glee. But the nex' week the same paper came out with another story, that a few years before, in Indiana, this man had been caught stealing a neighbor's sheep.

At this he became very angry and threatened to horsewhip the editor, and sue for damages, and everything else of the kind.

At this his wife said to him: "Why do you make such a fuss, Joel, over this little thing? It is not half nor a quarter as bad as the story they told about you last week."

"Why, the fact is, Maria, *this last story is true*; that is what makes me so mad about it."

I introduce this homely little incident because it so aptly illustrates one of the peculiar phases of human nature. Apply the lesson it illustrates to various persons and 'isms and you will quickly ascertain which ones are true and which false, or rather, I might say, those which are supported by facts and those which derive their support from mere assertions.

While the officers of this Grand Temple hold very decided views upon the subject of the re-enbodiment or re-incarnation of souls, and consequently teach the same in the advanced degrees, we do not take any offence whatever, if some of our members cannot agree with us. But, when any member feels that he cannot return the same courtesy to us, but feels antagonistic and inharmonious because others *do* believe, it is high time for that member to call a halt and ask himself *why he fears the teaching.* The answer may enlighten him a little.

It was the refusal of the Brothers of the O. O. M. to give countenance to the vain frivolities and wild, unfounded religious theories of the later Kings and Courts of Egypt, that caused their downfall and the destruction of their temples. Gorged with the luxuries of pomp and power, the later Kings and Queens from Darius I of the Twenty-seventh Dynasty, to Cleopatria the beautiful but ill-fated Queen, gradually lost their spiritulality and cared less for their souls and more for their bodies, until the entire court was permeated with luxurious sensuality.

Even the branch of the Magi that became Masonry at the building of King Solomon's Temple, have narrowly escaped annihilation many times because the order would not bend to the church in her most onerous exactions

The order of the Magi has come again to

the earth, to stay and work for the uplifting
and regeneration of man.   Its aims are to do
all the good possible, and to injure no one.
That we must, as of old, meet with enmity,
vituperation and false representation, is a
foregone conclusion.   We always have had
these to contend with and always shall have,
while poor humanity is on its present plane.

But we must press onward regardless of all
obstacles, and our crown of glory will be all
the brighter for our overcoming them.

ARTICLE I.

A Mysterious Tale.

OLNEY H. RICHMOND TELLS HOW HE BE-CAME A MEMBER OF THE MAGI.

His Experience at Nashville and Hair Breadth Escapes During the War - His Phil-osophy, His Religion - An Oath-Bound Society with Signs and Passwords - A Craft which Flourished 20,000 Years Before Christ -- Description of the Temple.

WONDER and much talk has been caused by several articles which have appeared in *The Democrat* recently, regarding occult astronomy, or astral magnetism, of which Olney H. Richmond. claims to be a student and expounder. Heretofore Mr. Richmond has refused to give a full

Introduction to Part 2.

Part II contains articles and extracts from newspapers, interviews and reports, which have appeared during the past two years, regarding the ORDER OF THE MAGI.

They throw so much light upon the question, and upon the manner in which the work had its start in the XIX Century, that many of our members had expressed a desire to have permanent copies of them for future reference.

Some portions of the interviews have been re-edited and curtailed somewhat, in order to eliminate matter that has ceased to be of interest since they were originally published, or of a local nature. Articles 1 and 2 from the *Grand Rapids Daily Democrat*, were published while I was a resident of Grand Rapids, Michigan. The others are taken from the *Progressive Thinker* of Chicago.

Olney H. Richmond.

account of the manner in which he became possessed of his mysterious knowledge. So much comment has been made on previous articles on the subject that Mr. Richmond was again called upon the other day and asked to give his story in full. His reason for refusing to give the information heretofore, was, as he said, because his superiors had not yet given him permission to tell. When accosted by the reporter the other day he answered cheerfully, " Come back here by the stove, where it is warm, and I will tell you the strange story of the manner in which I became acquainted with this wonderfully philosophy." This the reporter willingly did, and on getting comfortably seated Mr. Richmond proceeded as follows:

RICHMOND'S STRANGE STORY.

" During the war I was a soldier in the Fourteenth Michigan Infantry, and in the spring of '64 our regiment was quartered at Nashville, Tennessee. One night, about 8 o'clock, when I was on camp-guard duty, I saw a man approaching. I thought at first that he might be a spy, but immediately after I first saw him he spoke to me. I concluded

he could do me no harm as I was so near the
camp, and so I answered his salute. He came
up to me and said, ' your name is Richmond.'
' Right,' said I, suppossing that some of my
comrades had given him my name. ' And
your other name is Yenlo, continued the
stranger. ' There you are wrong, for that is
not my name.' ' Yes, it is,' said he, ' at least
that is the name given you by my authorities,
who have sent me to you; spell Yenlo backward and see what you make of it.' ' O-l-n-e-y,
Olney; why, yes, that is my name.' ' Yes,
and you were born on February 22, in the
year 1844,' said the stranger. ' How did you
find that out?' ' By the wonderful philosophy which I wish to communicate to you. I
do not know you, but was guided to you. I
am a member of an order which has been lost
to the public for many ages; I am a member
of the ancient order of the Magi, which
flourished in Egypt thousands of years ago.

I feel that I am about to die, and am bound
by the powers that rule me to convey the marvelous secrets which I hold, to another, who
shall live after me. You are that successor,

and I wish you to call on me at No. — ——
street some evening, and very soon, for I am
sure that I shall not live long.' My curiosity
was aroused and I promised to do as he
wished me.

A VISIT TO THE STRANGER.

"The man was a tall, thin, hollow-cheeked
individual, and was very earnest in his conver-
sation.   I called on him as I had promised,
and he initiated me into the high order of
which I have the honor to be a member. He
also gave me different articles which are necessary in the study. He was a Frenchman
and told me that he had been told the secrets
in India.

"I did not understand but very little of
what he told me at the time, but I am now
able to understand it all, and the signs, passwords, etc., that he gave me really amounted
to initiation into the higher degrees of the
craft. 'I am much obliged to you,' said I to
him, 'for the information you have given me,
but it seems to me, inasmuch as the object is
to transmit this knowledge in an unbroken
line, you are leaving it in bad hands.' 'How

so?' said the Frenchman. I answered, 'How long the war will last I have no means of knowing; I am liable to be killed long before the war ends, and could not transmit this knowledge to another person.' He said: 'I am not acting without knowledge; you need not fear; you will pass through many battles hereafter, but without injury; not a bullet will touch you.'

HIS NARROW ESCAPES.

"I must confess that I did not believe what he told me, for before every battle that I ever took part in, I felt that I was about to be killed. But, sure enough, not an enemy's bullet touched my body, notwithstanding that my clothes were perforated in several instances. Something always seemed to move me just enough to escape a bullet. At Kenesaw, for instance, I was standing with my head above the breastworks, looking at the enemy's batteries on the mountain. Suddenly and involuntarily I ducked my head below the head-log just in time to escape a rifle-ball from a sharpshooter, coming from a direction in which I had not been looking. He had evi-

dently been taking deliberate aim at me. On
another occasion I was sitting on a bank, and
by some unaccountable impulse I suddenly
arose, just in time to escape a twenty-pound
shot which whizzed past right beneath my
coat skirts. This was at the siege f Atlanta.
I might relate many similar instances of this
character, but this will suffice to show you
that some unseen power constantly protected me.

IN THE HANDS OF FATE.

"At the close of the war I came North and
opened a store at Cedar Springs. I resided
there for several years, and removed my store
to Pierson, a small town a few miles north of
Cedar Springs. I was at this place in 1871,
and it was in this year that I took an unaccountable notion that I wanted to go to Chicago; I did not know why I wanted to go, but
something made me desire to go. My wife
asked me if I was going there to buy goods

I told her no, I could buy all the goods I
wanted in Grand Rapids, but that I needed re-
laxation and had made up my mind that I
would take it in Chicago. I went, and as I

intended to stay for some time, went to a private boarding house, at, I think, 172 State street. I do not know why I went to this particular house, but I was attracted to it. There were several boarders in the same house, and at the first meal I took there I met a gentleman with whom I immediately formed an attachment. His name was Dr. Hamilton, from Charleston, South Carolina. After we had finished the meal we had a cigar together and got to talking. He invited me up to his room, and while we were there he showed me some books, among which was an old book, which he said was a family heirloom. He had no idea why he had brought the book along with him when he came to Chicago to seek his fortune. I opened the book and was surprised to see some of the mysterious words which the Frenchman had given me at Nashville seven years before.

THE MYSTERIES UNLOCKED.

"My curiosity was at once aroused, and I concluded that I could spare as much as $25 to buy that book, if it could be bought for that sum. I asked him how much he would

take for it. 'I have no use for it' said he, 'take
it along if you want it.' I brought the book
home with me and it cast a flood of light on
my studies. which I began to prosecute with
great vigor. It took me from that time to
this, over eighteen years of profound study
for me to gain the valuable knowledge which
I now possess. I have books which have cost
a great deal of money and labor to produce.
As you observe, they are mostly printed by
hand, with rubber stamps and only two sets
of these books exist on this earth. It took
years to get them up.

"Are you a Mason?" asked he of the
reporter.

"No sir I am not."

"I was going to say, if you were I could
give you a much better idea of my philosophy.
The Masonic order claims to have had its origin among the ancient priests of Iris. My
philosophy is the true Masonry; that which
existed among the ancient Chaldeans 20,000
years before Christ. Every Mason will admit
that a great change took place in the order at
the time of the building of Solomon's temple.

The 'word' which is so often mentioned in the bible, was lost at that time, and the 'word' is the great secret of the order. To this day no one outside the Magi knows what this word is. My philosophy is really my religion."

"Does your religion include a Christ?"

"Most certainly it does; my religion is the true Christianity. Christ was a member of the Magi and received his education at the hands of the order when he went down into Egypt. Why is the fact of Christ receiving his education in Egypt spoken of so little in the bible? Simply because, as it now is, it reached the present generation with many of the books suppressed. It is because of the church that the arts of the Magi have been suppressed so many hundreds of years. The exponents of the craft have been burned at the stake by the church and tortured to death in many other ways, so that the order has been kept very secret, no one but the members dreaming of its existence. One proof to Christians of the truth of astrology is the fact that the three wise men who found Christ in

the manger at Bethlehem were guided thither
by a star. These three wise men were a committee from the Magi. The old prophets
mentioned in the bible were members of the
Magi, and foretold coming events by the stars
and planets.

"My religion does not require that its believers shall have faith. Where Christians, that is
Christians in the common acceptation of the
word, believe in a heaven and have faith that
there is one; I know and have absolute proof
that there is one. By "heaven" I do not mean
a place where winged angles sit about on a
cloud, playing golden harps, but a practical
hereafter, a heaven such as a man makes for
himself. A man of high and refined tastes
certainly would not be happy in a heaven
where he would be classed with men of naturally low tastes."

"Now that the church has been wrested
from its throne of temporal power, so that it
cannot materially interfere with worldly
affairs, it is time the ancient order of the
Priests of Isis should be revived, and within
the past year I have been directed by the

powers who rule me to communicate my knowledge to others. Accordingly I have formed a class, which already includes thirty members, many of them prominent and influential men and women, who are cultured and refined people."

"Then you admit ladies to your secrets?" was asked.

"Yes sir; in the ancient days such was not the case, but women now stand on a level with men and they are admitted. It is not an easy thing to become a member of our circle, and many applications have been denied. Members must stand well, intellectually and socially, and withall be virtuous, else they will be unable to grasp the great ideas of this philosophy. An oath-bound order is the result of the formation of my class, several members of which reside in other parts of the state, and one lives as far away as the state of Alabama. We have a room all fitted up for our temple, which is located on this street. We have our signs, passwords, etc., and symbols and articles similar to those used by the Priests af Isis, way back in the time

of the Rameses and Pharaohs. We have
elected officers and no outsiders are admitted
at our meetings."

A VISIT TO THE TEMPLE.

At Mr. Richmond's invitation, the writer
visited the temple. The first thought that
strikes the mind of the visitor on entering the
place, is that he is in an astronomical study,
and such is the case, except that the place is
devoted more to the occult branches of the
study rather than plain astronomy. In the
center of the ceiling is a large elliptical diagram, which includes the signs of the zodiac,
and from the center of the figure is suspended
a large white globe, which represents the sun.

Within this globe are several incandescent
electric lights, one or all of which can be
turned on, and any shade of light obtained
which is desired. Around the sun, at relative
distances and locations, are suspended the
planets. By means of this system all manner
of astronomical phenomena can be plainly illustrated. The walls are hung with charts of
the heavens and illustrations of planetary
movements. Four chairs evidently for the

officers of the temple, are stationed opposite each other on the four sides of the room. Against one of the chairs, presumably that of one of the officers, leaned the symbol of his office, the three-pronged spear of Neptune. Mr. Richmond explained that this trident was

THE OLDEST SYMBOL KNOWN

on the earth at the present time. It was the emblem of the ancient lost Atlantis, and was derived by tl en from the form in which the stars now composing the Great Dipper of the North occupied 22.0 0 years ago, as has recently been demonstrated with the spectroscope by mathematical calculation based upon the motion of the seven stars composing the tail and part of the body of the Great Bear.

As descriptions have heretofore been related of Mr. Richmond's mysterious performances, it will not be necessary to describe seeming miracles which he performed during this visit to his temple.

Mr. Richmond says he does not mean to antagonize prevailing religions with his philosophy: all that he antagonizes is their dogmas. His philosophy, he claims, give as much clearer insight into true Christianity. Several Masons are among his most ardent students.

Mr. Richmond claims that his studies show that the Order of the Magi existed and was started on the continent of Atlantis, which existed in the Atlantic Ocean too many ages gone by for man to trace back. This is where he thinks the Garden of Eden was located—on the continent which he believes sank beneath the waves ages upon ages before the time that the first page of history begins to record the accurate story of mankind.

ARTICLE II.

Magnetism of Stars.

A STUDENT REVIEWS AN ANCIENT MYSTERY.

HIS INTERESTING EXPLORATIONS IN THE REALM OF
OCCULT ASTRONOMY WONDERFUL FEATS PER-
FORMED THROUGH THE AGENCY OF ORIENTAL
THEOREMS HE CAN DELINEATE A PERSONS HOR-
OSCOPE BY MATHEMATICAL PROCESSES—A TALK
WITH THE MAGICIAN.

ESIDING quietly in this city,
to all outward appearances per-
suing a simple and uneventful
life of a business man, dwells a
student of the ancient arts of
magic practiced by the Egyptians,
Chaldeans and other Eastern people
prior to the opening of the Christian era.

This gentleman, for many years, has been secretly delving into those scientific mysteries which for ages have been kept veiled from the world, passing only, he says, down the generations by word of mouth from frater to frater under the pledge of secrecy of which death was the penalty. The gentleman, Olney H. Richmond, has now acquired a knowledge that enables him to accomplish

FEATS IN OCCULTISM

that to the uninitiated seem fabulous and impossible. He has given evidences of his ability which to the cultured are remarkable and inexplicable.

Since those days when the Sphinx was given shape to pass down the ages (with mute lips) which hid knowledge of things passed away, and the Pyramids were built and locked with a key to unsolvable riddles, which some vengeful priest hurled into the muddy Nile, the mysteries of the arts of the ancients have ever been a source alike of interest and skepticism to scientists. Mr. Richmond claims that he has *found the golden key,* and has unlocked these fathomless mysteries.

He says he has already found and proven much, and is occupied with a course of study, the end of which he can now only conjecture.

Mr. Richmond entertained a reporter of *The Democrat* for a few hours yesterday He was found in his study surrounded by astronomical charts and diagrams, together with a large assortment of occult books and symbolical wheels containing zodiacal signs.

"I do not wish newspaper notoriety," Mr. Richmond explained, "for my studies have been private, and I have never had any idea of using them in any way for publicity or profit." The reporter urged him to tell

SOMETHING OF HIS HOBBY,

remarking that he had already given one or two private exhibitions to friends, which had created a great amount of interest. At length Mr. Richmond gave out a little intelligence of the system used by him and made a couple of practical experiments illustrating the laws of Astral Magnetism (the name given it) and the part played therein by playing cards used as the emblems of planetary aspects and polarities. One of the books used in the

manifestations bore the following grandilo-
quent title: Astral Card Charts, Birth Tarots
and Planetary Culminations on the Heliocentric Projection. The book in size and binding
resembled a large family bible.

"My study," continued Mr. Richmond, "is
in line of one of the most ancient orders of Oriental occultism. An order that antedates even
Blue Lodge Masonry and dates back to the
time when the halls of great Balbec and proud
Karnac echoed to the footfalls of

PRIESTS AND NEOPHYTES.

Never, since the haughty kingdom of Atlantis
sank beneath the ocean, have the secrets of this
order been given to any but a chosen few.
Fostered by the kings of Egypt and religiously
perserved in the custody of the priesthood in
their temples, the arts known to the Magi
have come down to our day within the hands
of but a few in each generation. Its devotees
have secretly met in caves amid the mountains of India and Hindoostan, as well as in
other mystic countries, and

CERTAIN CABALISTIC FORMULA

have been thus handed down the ages, from

mouth to ear, to the present time. During the past seventeen hundred years each person receiving these teachings have been obliged by solemn oath to transmit them to some worthy and younger person that they may not be lost through failure of succession.

"Everything in this work is under strict mathematical laws," explained Mr. Richmond, "and the movements of the planets are traced with accuracy. even to a second of arc. Time is an important element in the calculations, as the revolution of the earth on its axis and its polar magnetism is calculated on a time basis."

Mr. Richmond has over two hundred "mysteries," which can be exhibited to prove his proposition. Among other feats he can delineate a person's horoscope and tell things about them they know, things they have forgotten. or are yet to know, the day they were born, year, month, and hour and all simply from the person's astral number.

Every person born into the world has a planet which especially rules over them and which during their span on earth, with the other bodies in the solar system plays an important part in shaping their lives. Each person, male or female, has an individual number drawn from the value of this overruling star, in these scientific calculations. This number is the basis for many of the mathematical wonders. Many of these "mysteries," Mr. Richmond asserts, can be easily mastered and elucidated by novices. The number 142857, so Mr Richmond informed the reporter, was a noted sacred number with the Egyptians, and has many wonderful mathematical and other properties. "These feats are not the work of spirits, psychology or hocus pocus, but simple magic, based on the laws of astronomy, as understood at the present time, aided by the ancient methods handed down from Egyptian, Chaldaic and Arabian Magi, to which many logarithmic rules of more modern times, based upon the same grand principals, have been added."

ARTICLE III.

A Mystic Temple.

VISIT OF A REPORTER TO THE GRAND TEMPLE OF THE MAGI.

He Interviews Prof. Richmond, the Able Exponent of Astral Magnetism.

STARTLING REVELATION ON THE ANCIENT MAGI AND ORDER OF MASONRY—THE HEAVENS AND PLANETARY PHENOMENA REPRODUCED IN THE TEMPLE WITH A GORGEOUSNESS ALMOST INDESCRIBABLE—HIS THEORIES AND BOOKS A SOURCE OF GREAT WONDERMENT AND PROFUSE COMMENT.

N this city resides a gentleman whose learning, comprehension, ideas and advanced thoughts on matters appertaining to physical and occult Astronomy, have forced him into prominence, not only in the immediate vicinity of his residence, but also in

the State of his nativity and this nation. He
is a man of modest appearance, but imperious
in his dealings with subjects of which he is
a master.

In the issue of April 5th, *The Progressive
Thinker* republished an article from the *Daily
Democrat* the leading paper in Grand Rapids,
setting forth the religious views entertained
by Prof. Richmond, together with a cursory
description of *"The Mystic Temple"* over
which he presides, and discourses to a large
number of the most intellectual and influential citizens. Through the interest awakened,
and large amount of inquiry fostered by the
publication of this article upon the astrologi-
cal researches of Prof. Richmond, and his rev-
elations from the standpoint of a student of
Occult Astronomy, we deemed it advisable to
send a reporter to interview the gentleman.

Having learned that he was to be found at
the Temple and that no meeting was being
held on this evening, the reporter proceeded
to the place where the Temple is situated and
the Master Mystic and his family reside. Mr.
Richmond was in his Temple, surrounded

with Mystic charts of all kinds and at work upon complicated mathematical formula appertaining to Astronomy. What strikes a visitor most upon entering this Temple of wonders, is the fact he sees before him the *Solar System*, in a more comprehensive and tangible shape than he has ever before seen.

The entire hall, from end to end, is filled with heavenly bodies, tilted at various angles to the plane of the ecliptic, thus illustrating their polarites, while at the same time various satellites revolve about their primaries, with their orbits inclined, as in Nature's realm of wonders. On the reporter introducing himself and business, Mr. Richmond laid aside his work and willingly gave all the information that he lawfully could divulge, relating to the order. "This large red planet with four moons or satellites, is Jupiter," said he, pointing to a globe about seven inches in diameter. You will notice that the satellites move in orbits, in a plane with their primary, while those of some other planets are widely divergent. For instance, you notice that this planet, Uranus, has four satellites

revolving in orbits at nearly right angles to
the ecliptic. This has been brought about
through the gradual change of their plane
during untold millions of years. This change
has proceeded in the case of Uranus, until
the tilt is at more than right angles, so
that the motion of the moons is actually
retrograde."

"Is this the only case of the kind in our
Solar System?" was asked.

"No! Here you see the planet Neptune
the far off sentinel of our System, has only
one moon. But this planet is so much older
than Uranus, that the tilting of the system
has gone on until it has actually turned
completely over, so it is nearly in the plane
of the ecliptic again; but of course, the motion is retrograde."

"I hardly understand that."

"Then let me explain. Take your hat and
revlove it in the direction of the hands of
a watch; there, now gradually tilt it over
until it is bottom up, still keeping up the revolution. Now you notice that the rim revolves
precisely retrograde to what it did before."

"Exactly! I understand it now, as I never could before."

"Here you see the great planet Saturn, with its rings and eight satellites, said Mr. Richmond, pointing to a glistening globe, suspended in midair by invisible wires and surrounded by several polished globes at various distances.

As the large electric *sun* in the center of the room lighted them, the globes glistened in the artificial sunlight. The reporter noticed an eclipse of two of Saturn's moons while one satellite made an eclipse on its primary at the same time. The reporter never realized before so completely how these phenomena occured.

"These small moons revolving so rapidly about Mars, are the little bodies *Dread* and *Terror*. This inner one enjoys the distinction of having the shortest year of any body in our system. Its year is seven hours, while its day is about twenty minutes long, as near as can be found. Think of an afternoon only five minutes in duration."

"It would hardly pay a fellow to go and

see his girl there, would it? If the lovers sat up till midnight they would only have about five minutes," said the reporter.

"I am glad I do not live there."

Mr. Richmond then showed the reporter several magnificent books bound in Russia, with gilt edges and sides. These books contained several hundred colored charts of the heavens, for all sorts of times and culminations. The explanations given of them were too long for a newspaper report, but they were most interesting.

"What are the fundamental laws that govern your occult work?" asked the reporter.

"The laws are few and simple," replied the Professor. "Here they are: For the want of a better name, we call this force that exists in the universe, Astral Magnetism. Some call it the soul in nature. It matters not whether it is called Magnetism, The Infinite, The Great I Am, God, Allah, or Mumbo Jumbo, it is the same great intelligent force, recognized by nearly all mankind. Now, the theory of our order is, that this great infinite force acts through regular laws, mathematically, accurate, and unchangeable. In short, that everything in the universe is governed by Law. Not even a crystal can form within a chemical combination, or anything however small, except under exact mathematical laws. The same laws that govern a grain of sand, governs that giant *Jupiter*, eighty-eight thousand miles in diameter."

"Are any of these laws formulated?"

"Hundreds of them are recorded in these books. Here we have a few which you may copy:

LAWS OF ASTRAL MAGNETISM.

1. "Every particle of matter in the universe acts upon every other particle, with a magnetic force directly proportional to its mass, and inversely to the square of its distance."

2. "The Astral Magnetism of all bodies, or aggregations of matter, varies according to the chemical constitution of the bodies."

3. "The intensity of the Astral force, and its lines of effect, vary according to the angles of polarity of the various bodies."

"These are the three first laws, and lay the foundation, so to speak, of all the other laws contained in these four books. Law No. 1 explains itself. No. 2 means that a globe of chloride of sodium, and, by the way, there are such in the Universe, has a magnetic effect on other matter, differing in quality from a globe composed of iron principally, granite, or any mixture of elements. No. 3 is more difficult to explain, but still very important; in fact, the importance of polarity is everything, in this Heliocentric Astrology. It is calculated by the hundreds of tables of logarithms you see in this book No. 1, which gives angles and change of polar force for all the planets, and the Earth, in all parts of the six orbits."

Is this astrology then different from that usually known and practiced?" asked the reporter.

"Most certainly it is, vastly different, from the Geocentric Astrology of the middle ages. There is as much difference as between modern chemistry and the alchemy of the middle ages. Heliocentric Astrology is based upon the true motion of the planets. Geocentric Astrology upon the false theory sustained by

Ptolemy and his followers. This theory was the only one allowed during the dark ages, every one being put to death, or thrown into a dungeon who ventured to dispute it. This is what caused the Magi to promulgate their true knowledge in a secret manner."

"What connection has your order with Masonry."

"Simply this: Three Masters of the outer circle, duly raised to the sublime degree, where they could be trusted with the *Word*, were educated in all the arts of the Magi, and after taking a solem oath, departed to a far country to found a Temple. The *Word* was divided into three parts, each one of the three receiving one of these parts, and they could not be put together except under certain astronomical laws; and that could only be done in the Holy of Holies, behind the three veils and upon the Altar. By the by, let me remark that, even to this day the *Word* can not be given, so that it will be of any use to the person receiving it, except under the same conditions. It may seem strange to you, *but* it is a cold *fact*."

"How then did it benefit you, when given

under the circumstances you have heretofore related?"

"It did not. I could not use it until the time arrived when an Altar could be made and dedicated, by placing thereon certain things that I can not mention. But hold on, I have lost the thread of my story. The three wise men I spoke of went to the country whence they came and began a Temple. But now came trouble. In those days bookkeeping was not understood as at present. How were one hundred and fifty-three thousand workmen of different grades, drawing different wages, to be handled and paid their weekly stipends? By a happy thought these officers resolved to use the organization plan, and make the workmen members of their secret order. But all those fit to cut stone and work on the Temple were not suitable persons to become members of the order that had in its keeping the learning and lore of past ages. To obviate this trouble, the three officers changed the initiative ceremonies and the minor passwords to conform to the religion of the Nation where the Temple was built. They intended however, when the Temple was finished, to then pick out the ones most worthy, and regularly initiate them into the original and seemingly incomprehensible mysteries of Egypt and Chaldea.

But alas, before the Temple was completed one of the three, Hiram Abiff, was murdered by some of the workmen, who in vain tried to extort from him the secret of the *Word*. Over his grave the other officers gave up all attempts to recover the lost *Word*, and adopted a substitute. Thus Modern Masonry was born. When I say modern, I mean it is modern compared with the great antiquity of what preceded it as an order."

"Why, the time the emblem of this order was adopted, from the stars that glistened in the great Bear, which was then in the form of this silver trident, was so long ago that the building of Solomon's Temple was as a thing of yesterday in comparison."

"Why did the officers not return, or send to Egypt and obtain the missing part of the sacred *Word?*"

"They did try to procure it, after time had elapsed and the Temple was completed.   But in the meantime the Magi had learned that the new order was so thoroughly changed that it had but a few of the astronomical features remaining, whereupon they refused to impart the secret."

"I have understood that the Masonic order afterwards found the *Word*."

"Yes, a great many have understood that, in modern times, but every advanced student of the history of the order knows that the Chapter and Temple degrees have all been invented and engrafted upon the original Blue-lodge in modern times. The alleged *Word*, found amid the ruins of the Temple, has no occult meaning, and cannot be fitted to the great truths of astronomy and time, as can the true *Word*."

"Do you then consider that your order militates against Masonry?"

"Not in the least. Masonry still stands on its own merits as an institution. The change made by King Solomon was no doubt a wise one, under all the circumstances existing at the time, and the Masonic institution has fulfilled its alloted place in the world. As a proof of this, we have in this order ardent Masons of 32 degrees, and many Blue-lodge and Chapter Masons."

MASONS THE MOST INTERESTED.

"Look at this pile of letters received from all parts of the country. You will notice that nine out of ten of them make some symbol such as a slipper, rope, tent, keystone, square and compass or else sign their communications, 'Yours Fraty.' All such are Masons. By the way, I will say, that no doubt many of these correspondents have been disappointed at not receiving answers. But I cannot spare the time to write so many letters, being busy with my necessary work for our Secret Order, which I find the regular duties of, consume much more time than one would suppose."

"The Light," resumed Mr. Richmond, "cannot be sent out to these distant friends, but I am going to do all that is within my power to do, in the way of sending out printed lectures and teachings for the benefit of these Mystic enquirers in other States, in order to prepare them for the time when they can come to the Temple.

"I would like to witness some of your occult work, Professer, if not against your rules."

"Oh! that would be all right. But it is quite late now for any demonstrations. If you will give me your exact date of birth, however, I will show you something at some future time."

The reporter gave his birth date, and promised to call again, when he hopes to lay before the readers of *The Progressive Thinker* something of great interest to students of Occultism.

ARTICLE IV.

Magical Wonders.

ANOTHER VISIT TO THE TEMPLE.

Explanation of Cards — Their Ancient Origin and Uses.

Prognostications Fulfilled on the Spot.

CARDS AS ASTRONOMICAL EMBLEMS—STRANGE PRO-
PERTIES OF PLAYING CARDS—GYPSIES HAVE
PRESERVED TRADITIONS OF THEIR MAGICAL
QUAALITIES—MATHEMATICAL DEMONSTRATIONS —
EGYPTIAN MAGIC AT THE DOORS OF THE PRAC-
TICAL XIX CENTURY.

IN the reporter's second visit to the Temple of the Magi, made a few days subsequent to the one narrated heretofore, he was met at the inner door by Mr. Richmond, who evidently was expecting him.

"Now, what investigations do you wish to make this evening?" inquired the professor.

" What I want most," replied the reporter, "is to witness some of the occult phenomena which I have seen accounts of in the papers; the Egyptian card mysteries and other exhibitions, such as you have given on several occasions."

"Before showing you these mysteries," said the Professor, "allow me to give you an insight into the history of playing cards. Generally, the very name of 'playing cards' brings out a sneer on the face of most people, who have visions come before their eyes of gambling rooms, drinking and late hours, or thoughts of tricksters and legerdemain. Now this is not to be wondered at, considering how cards have been used for hundreds of years past. But, on the other hand, ask those who have had most to do with cards, and you will find that, without knowing a single thing about the philosophy of it, every such person is a firm believer in 'lucky suits,' his 'lucky card' or his luck running good and poor at different times.

Now, at first sight, this looks like bosh to a thinking person, and I once thought so myself; but facts are stubborn things and will upset any number of fine-spun theories. For instance, take the theories of Ptolemy and his followers relating to the motion of the heavenly bodies. How quickly they had to fall before the facts discovered by Copernicus. I should say re-discovered though, for the same facts were well known thousands of years before Copernicus.

But I started to explain about cards. It has been claimed by many historians that the French invented them, about the fourteenth century or later, and that they were made to play games with and to amuse the French court and people. Nothing could be farther from the truth than this account of their origin and purposes. If they were so invented, why is it that the court cards bear upon their faces even to this day, not only the likenesses of ancient kings, queens and courtiers of Egypt, but also secret symbols of the Magi and priests of Isis?

These symbols have been handed down and reproduced by each generation of engravers and printers, as it were, unconsciously.

The wandering tribes of Gypsies have preserved the secrets of cards as emblems of planetary motion, time, etc., without having preserved the higher knowledge that enables us to explain why and how it is that they have these properties.

I am myself of the opinion that playing cards had their origin even farther back than Egypt. Even upon the Island of Atlantis, a remnant of what was once an immense continent where the ocean now rolls.

But, let this be as it may, they were used by the Egyptian priests in their sacred astronomical mysteries, as abundant evidence shows. They regarded them as sacred emblems of astronomical time, and combinations of the solar system.

Says Ammon, ' The religion of the Egyptians was wholly based on astronomy, and these cards were constructed with perfect mathematical and symbolical reference to time, planetary motion, and the occult calculations and mysteries of the Magi. Thus the fifty-two cards correspond to the weeks in a year. The court cards to the months and signs of the zodiac. The three court cards symbolize in each suit

the three houses of one-quarter of the zodiac.
Hearts in the first quarter symbolize spring.
also love and friendship. Clubs in the second
quarter, summer; also knowledge, learning,
religion, heat, temper, quarrels, law suits, etc.

Diamonds in the third quarter symbolize
fall. when the crops are gathered and sold, and
therefore represent wealth, power and trade.
Spades rule in the fourth quarter, and stand
or winter. cold, darkness, death, hardship,
labor, etc.

Every aspect has its ruling or emblematic
card, and every day and year its ruling card.
Even the minutes have each a card called the
'minute card of time.'

In ancient times they only recognized three
hundred and sixty-four days to the year, the
odd day being regarded as waste time, and used
up in pleasure and amusement. Now, as each
card rules a day under each of the seven
planets during a year, you can see that they
exactly fill out the year, seven times fifty-two
making 364.

ANTIQUITY OF PLAYING CARDS.

Even to this day we have no ruling card for

the 31st of December, and I cannot perform many of the mysteries in these books on that day in consequence. The ancients, it is true, knew not the existence of Neptune and Uranus, but they counted the sun and moon as planets, which made up the seven.

You know seven has always been a sacred number among all nations and in all religions, the center, so to speak of all symbolic numbers.

The seven is also the center of each of the four suits of cards, whether counting from the king or from the ace. The thirteen cards of each suit is also astronomical and indicates among other things, knowledge of good and evil.

That is why, I suppose, that thirteen has been assigned to the 'Old Boy.' in the same category with the printing press and other wicked things, and regarded as unlucky.

The Magi of ancient times knew that the time would come when their sacred emblems would be prostituted to base uses. They predicted that the time would come when 'these sacred emblems will be trampled under the feet of the ungodly, and become a reproach

in high places, although, through all coming
time, amid downfalls of empires, and kings,
these emblems shall go on unchanged in
value and effect.'"

"It is singular," continued Mr. R., "but it
is a fact, that many and many a time inven-
tors and manufactures have endeavored to
introduce packs of cards containing more or
less in number, or with a change in the emblems used. But in every case they have
met with a flat failure; fifty-two they were,
and fifty-two they remain to this day.

The card called a Joker, introduced in late
years, amounts to nothing. Its value is a
cypher astronomically, and although placed
in every pack made lately, it is thrown away
by the purchaser as soon as he sees it. Still
it rules on that odd day I mentioned to you,
as you can prove by rule No. 1 in this book
upon the Altar.

"But we will now come to some practical
work, which will illustrate the occult powers
of cards better than a hundred pages of argument would do," said Mr. Richmond, looking
at his watch. "I have made a few prognosti-

cations for this occasion which are contained in this sealed letter and this record book and now is the time for them to be fulfilled."

Then followed some of the most astonishing exemplifications of the strange and even marvelous properties of those little pieces of pasteboard, that could be imagined.

Not to go into minute particulars, we will simply say, that prognostications made and sealed the day before, were fulfilled in the smallest particulars and the reporter found for the first time in his life, that no such thing apparently as "chance" exists. He also found that through all the handling and mixing which he gave them, they preserved a strange and unmistakable shadowing of his life which came out under the planetary laws in such a way as to show things that had happened and others that were to come; known only to the reporter himself.

It is useless, however, to give descriptions of these occult, or magic manifestations, for no man can understand or appreciate them without seeing them for himself.

The reporter had in a measure been prepared for some wonderful manifestations, but he had not really at heart believed it possible.

Two other mysteries were then exhibited, the reporter performing the mathematical work himself, but full details are too long to insert in this article.

"Now, Professor," said the reporter, "as what I have seen, illustrating the laws of planetary effects upon luck and chance, so-called, has been so satisfactory, I would be pleased to see some other manifestations illustrating the occult powers of the Magi."

Mr. Richmond then gave the reporter one or two other private exhibitions of white magic, which were strange and marvelous and seemed to take one back to the days of Moses, Aaron and King Pharoah.

"These Oriental mysteries have been changed from age to age to suit the different circumstances and environments of the time," resumed Mr. Richmond "knowledge of nature's laws confers new powers and conditions upon later generations of men, and relegates to the domain of recognized science other powers formerly deemed occult."

"To illustrate: Nowadays the powers of psychology, mesmerism, hypnotism and kindred manifestations of mind transference are well known and recognized by the scientific world, so that phenomena based upon these powers are no longer 'mysterious' and therefore not 'magical.' Consequently, the great feats performed by Moses and other Magicians in ancient times are of no use now in the advancement of mankind to higher planes of thought.

If the Magicians of Egypt should now appear before our President in such a Snake Contest as they gave before the king of Egypt ages ago, the President would say, 'very good, very good indeed, these exhibitions of psychological powers are very interesting' and he would be right."

"Take the power of healing diseased conditions of the flesh by magnetic passes, mind force, or laying on of hands. This is getting to be nearly as common now, as bleeding and blistering used to be fifty years ago.

Jesus had this power, but he belonged. from the age of twelve, to what was known as the Essenene branch of the Magi, who believed more in elevation of the soul at the expense of the body, than in cultivating the intellectual forces.

His phenomenal powers took direction accordingly. Some of the Magi naturally developed one way, and others another, as all cannot be alike.

Jesus the wise—had his elders or twelve deciples of the outer circle, all with him during his travels, but not one developed into the same power as the master.

Perhaps if he had lived to found a temple at Jerusalem, as he wished to do, they would have become more fully developed."

With many thanks for kindness extended, the reporter left, with a promise to call again.

TO OUR READERS.

EXTRACTS FROM THE PROGRESSIVE THINKER,

Published at 40 Loomis St., Chicago, Illinois.

Our old subscribers will remember that *The Progressive Thinker* was made the official organ of the Order of the Magi about one year and a half ago, when Prof. Richmond and his family were preparing to come to Chicago to enter upon their great work. Since that time various lectures have appeared therein, together with short bulletins occasionally, regarding the work. The Order being secret, it follows as a matter of course, that many of our subscribers cannot fully realize its nature or the full scope of the occult knowledge therein imparted; on the other hand, there is a large number who are in full sympathy with the work of Prof. Richmond, in the study of those occult forces, the existence of which can be demonstrated in a hundred different ways in the Temple of the Magi, at 1910 Washington Boulevard, and to them this number of *The Progressive Thinker* will prove a great attraction.

In no sense does the Order of the Magi conflict with those laws that underlie true Spiritualism or its phenomena; it is, in fact, in complete harmony therewith, but it extends its domain of action to those occult forces that are interblended with, and are a part of our planetary system, and which nowhere else on this earth receive a full and complete interpretation.

While *The Progressive Thinker* is devoted to the promulgation of modern Spiritualism, its phenomena and philosophy. it will continue to occasionally sandwich in its columns articles and movements that are of vital interest to the great mass of Spiritualists, and in regard to which they should be familiar. As a member of the Order of the Magi, as one who has carefully and critically examined the details of its workings, and seen time and time again a demonstration of the existence of occult forces which seem to be imbued with intelligence, we are prepared to speak understandingly.

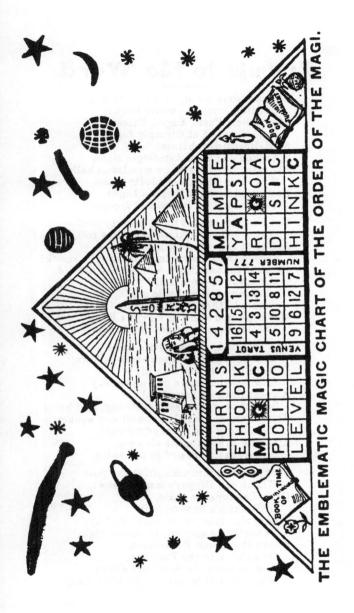

THE EMBLEMATIC MAGIC CHART OF THE ORDER OF THE MAGI.

Tribute to the Word.

Oh wondrous Word, now lost to man;
  Existing since the world began;
Thy power; Poets, Sages, Priests;
  Hath chanted at Olympic feasts,
At Heliopolistic shrines,
  Arched o'er with Astrologic signs,
Beneath proud Karnac's wondrous halls,
  Within great Balbec's lofty walls.
Embodied in their Tripple Light
  You flashed on Priest and Neophite.

But now, where art thou, mighty soul—
  Where hidest thou as Centuries roll,
Art thou engraved on hidden rock
  Secure from storm and earthquake shock?
Canst thou look down where thou art hid,
  From top of some tall Pyramid?
Or doth some Monolithic shaft
  Withhold thee from Masonic Craft?
Mayhap some tomb of Egypt's Race
  Enfolds thee in its cold embrace.

Thy syllables, three mystic links
  May be engraved upon some Sphinx
Or shining ever from on high,
  Enscrolled in stars on yonder sky.
A great Philosopher of old
  Said thou wert massive, strong, and bold;
That thou wert neither round nor square,
  Yet beauty had, exceeding rare,
A beauty that delights all eyes;
  So mayhap thou *art* in the skies.

Perhaps thou circumscrib'st the pole
  Within the Dipper's mighty bowl,
Or in Cassiopeia's chair,
  Or Bernice's flowing hair.
Where e'er thou art in Earth or Sky,
  Beneath the ground, or set on high,
Above the frozen Polar Seas,
  Or shining in the Pleiades,
Or nailed unto the Southern Cross.
  Where e'er thou art, we feel thy loss.

Recognition.

INSCRIBED TO THE ORDER OF THE MAGI.
By Geo. P. McIntyre.

Principals rise no higher than their source.
Law rules the spheres and ever was in force.
From globe-the-atom, to globe-the-largest sun;
All through the interstices the laws impelling run.
And through each atom vibrant with control;
The same is manifest as in the axial pole.
Law cannot err; its mandates are absterse;
Involving all activity throughout the universe.
"Omnipotence" would be meaningless; "Omniscience"
    the same;
If law did not co-ordinate to vindicate this claim.
Law differentiates and runs with evoluting pace;
From animalcule to man; the father of his race.
Law thrilled his nostrils with inspiration rife;
Drawn from boundless reservoirs of Eternal Life!
It gave to him an intellect to recognize its course;
And the finite times the Infinite prescient to its source.
Something from nothing never did exist;
Spirit is magnetic which no thing can resist.
It is this quickning essence which permates the whole;
And man builds on Truth the epitome of the soul.
    Chicago July 1892

Drop Your Bucket.

By S. W. Foss.

"Oh, ship ahoy!" rang out the cry:
"Oh, give us water or we die!"
A voice came o'er the waters far,
"Just drop your bucket where you are,"
And then they dipped and drank their fill
Of water fresh from mead and hill;
And then they knew they sailed upon
The broad mouth of the Amazon.

O'er tossing wastes we sail and cry,
"Oh, give us water or we die!"
On high relentless waves we roll
Through arid climates for the soul;
'Neath pitiless skies we pant for breath,
Smit with the thirst that drags to death,
And fail, while faint for fountains far,
To drop our buckets where we are.

On, ship ahoy! your sailing on
The broad mouth of the Amazon,
Whose mighty currents flows and sings
Of mountain streams and inland springs,
Of night-kissed morning's dewy balm,
Of heaven-dropt evening's twilight calm,
Of nature's peace in earth or star—
Just drop your bucket where you are.

Seek not for fresher founts afar,
Just drop your bucket where you are;
And while the ship right onward leaps,
Uplift it from exhaustless deeps.
Parch not your lips with dry despair;
The stream of hope flows everywhere.
So, under every sky and star,
Just drop your bucket where you are.

CPSIA information can be obtained at www.ICGtesting.com
Printed in the USA
BVOW11s1213250614

357339BV00012B/822/P